Using the Bible
in Groups

Using the Bible in Groups

Roberta Hestenes

The Westminster Press
Philadelphia

First published 1983 in Great Britain by Bible Society, Swindon, Wilts
(ISBN 0 564 07032 7)

Unless otherwise stated, Bible text is from the *Good News Bible*
(British edition)
© American Bible Society, New York, 1966, 1971, 1976.

"Eight covenant dynamics" reprinted by permission from *Covenant to Care*
by Louis H. Evans, Jr. Published by Victor Books, Wheaton, Illinois.

"Inductive Study" from *How to Start a Neighborhood Bible Study* by Marilyn
Kunz and Catherine Schell. Published by Tyndale House Publishers, Inc.,
© 1973 Marilyn Kunz and Catherine Schell. Used by permission.

"Leadership Styles" based on ideas from *Building Small Groups in the
Christian Community* by John Mallison, Renewal Publications, Australia, ©
1978 John Mallison.

First American edition

Published by The Westminster Press®
Philadelphia, Pennsylvania

PRINTED IN THE UNITED STATES OF AMERICA
9 8 7 6 5 4 3 2 1

Library of Congress Cataloging in Publication Data

Hestenes, Roberta.
  Using the Bible in groups.

  Bibliography: p.
  Includes indexes.
  1. Church group work. 2. Bible—Study. I. Title.
BV652.2.H47 1985   268'.6   84-15291
ISBN 0-664-24561-7 (soft)

I would like to thank my husband, John, my assistant, Jollene Anderson, and my mentor, Glen Barker, the Provost of Fuller.

Contents

1

Why Small Groups?

To open the Bible is to begin an adventure, a journey of discovery. This adventure has been going on for thousands of years as God has made himself known to men and women, children and young people, calling them to a new and meaningful life rooted and centred in love. The Bible tells us the story of God's mighty words and actions. As we read and listen, we discover that we are invited to become participants in this great drama of redemption and forgiveness, of power and promise, of courage and comfort. To seek to know this story better and discover our own place in it, we study the Bible. And because this story is the tale of a people, a community of faith, we find it helpful to read with others – to study the Bible in groups.

Positive change
For nearly two thousand years Christians have been meeting together in small groups to study the Bible. Sometimes the meetings are disappointing. More often men and women have discovered a closeness to God and their lives have been transformed through their involvement with small groups of Christians. In a wide variety of settings and circumstances, from sanctuary to sitting room, in catacombs and gulags, Bible study in groups has been a major ingredient in the spread and vitality of the Christian faith.

On the increase
Throughout the world today there is a widespread increase in the variety and number of small Bible study groups.

When western Christians were first able to visit China after the country had been isolated for many years, they wanted answers to many questions. Had the Christians managed to survive with the expulsion of missionaries, the shutdown of centres of worship and the persecution which was sometimes very harsh? The news from China today is staggering. Not only has the church survived, it has actually grown. How is this possible? Home fellowships! Christians in China by the hundreds of thousands have met in small informal home gatherings for worship, Bible study and prayer. In these settings they have found strength and courage to continue in their Christian faith. In some Latin American countries as recently as twenty years ago, ordinary individuals were not encouraged to study the Bible for themselves. Today there are thousands of Roman Catholic and Protestant small group Bible studies. In the last twenty years, in Great Britain and in America, there has been an explosive increase in the number and variety of ways in which lay Christians meet together to learn more about their Christian faith and how it applies to their personal and communal life.

THE BENEFITS OF SMALL GROUPS

We need Christian small groups because they help us to become what we are meant to be – those set free by the love of Christ, who seek to share his love with others.

Meeting needs

Christian small groups can meet some of the most important needs that we have:

- O the need for spiritual growth
- O the need for friendship, support and encouragement
- O the need for strength in the face of temptation and trial
- O the need to give and receive love
- O the need to serve others.

Understanding and responding, in faith, to the Word of God is the foundation of all Christian life and action. As Christians we are told: "Do not conform yourselves to the standards of this world, but let God transform you inwardly by a complete change of your mind" (Romans 12.2). Small groups which use the Bible as part of their life together can enable this transformation and renewal to take place. This can result in benefits for individuals, for the church and for society.

Lay leadership

During periods of renewal in Church history, small groups have been one of the ways in which vital personal faith in Jesus Christ has been nurtured and encouraged. Small groups have been used in order to help people to discover for themselves what the Bible says and what it means to be a Christian and to participate in the Christian community. They have been used as a means for the church to reach beyond itself to those outside its active membership. Lay leadership emerges in small group involvement and the church is strengthened.

Social justice

In addition, people joining together in a small group have often helped to right the injustices and solve the problems present in their country at that time. For instance, William Wilberforce and a number of fellow Christians joined together in what came to be called the Clapham Sect. This group led Great Britain to abolish the slave trade and eventually to abolish slavery altogether.

THE CHURCH AS A CENTRE FOR COMMUNITY

Both within western culture and in the Church today there is a need to develop committed communities intent upon caring. Human beings created in the image of God find their meaning and purpose for life within the context of both divine and human fellowship. One of the first statements in the Bible concerning man says: "It is not good for the man to live alone" (Genesis 2.18). To be fully human requires participation in a relationship with God and with other people. This relationship involves knowing and being known, caring for others as well as being cared for. From the beginning when Jesus first called the twelve disciples to share his life and ministry, his followers found that their response to Jesus' invitation to follow him involved them in a community.

In company

The Christian life is not a solitary journey. It is a pilgrimage made in the company of the committed. The "new commandment" which Jesus taught his disciples was to "love one another". It is not enough to love God. Love of God calls us to love one another. The letters of the early Christian leaders were usually addressed to small groups of Christians, not to individuals. The groups were meeting in various places, often homes, throughout the far-flung cities of the Roman Empire. A recurrent theme in these early writings was the call to life together. A description of those first Christians who responded to the preaching of the apostle Peter at Pentecost says:

> Many of them believed his message and were baptized, and about three thousand people were added to the group that day. They spent their time in learning from the apostles, taking part in the fellowship, and sharing in the fellowship meals and the prayers . . . Day after day they met as a group in the Temple, and they had their meals together in their homes, eating with glad and humble hearts, praising God, and enjoying the good will of all the people.

(Acts 2.41-42, 46-47a)

Notice the relationship between the large group meeting together in the Temple and the small group gatherings in homes.

Balanced approach

Some contemporary Christian leaders express a concern that a strong emphasis on Christians meeting together in small groups to learn more about their faith, using the Bible as a resource, will result in a reduced commitment to the larger central gatherings of the church for worship and teaching. But it need not be a case of choosing one form of gathering over the other.

As we have seen from the example of the early Church, small groups can complement regular meetings of the whole congregation for worship and study. Both are necessary to the healthy functioning of a church. Each meets a need. The two sorts of gatherings should work together to build a strong community of Christian people. A small group that does not relate to a larger church body may suffer limitations or even distortions in its understanding of the Christian tradition. A large worshipping community without some type of small group involvement risks developing a fellowship which is friendly and polite on the surface but which may not discover the rich resources that arise from the membership being more deeply involved with one another.

One result of this pattern of life together is recorded for us: "And every day the Lord added to their group those who were being saved" (Acts 2.47b). Church growth resulted from the proclamation and reality of the gospel demonstrated in the vitality of life and caring in the new community of believers.

A job for the community

From those early days in the life of the Church, Christians down through the centuries have known they need each other for fellowship and to fulfill the purpose for which Christ called them into being. The mission of the Church to share the good news of the love of God is the responsibility both of individual Christians and of the Christian community.

When Christ sent out the first disciples on a mission into the towns and villages of Palestine, he did not send them out one by one. Rather, he chose a number to go, trained them as a group, then sent them out in pairs. Even in his own relationship with the Twelve, Jesus had a special relationship with three of the men, and beyond that circle, Scripture tells us, he had special friends in Mary, Martha and Lazarus. Jesus lived his own life in community. He instructed his followers about how to live life in community.

The early Church spread like wildfire throughout the world as bands of Christians shared their lives and ministry together in response to the love and purpose of God. They spoke of themselves as a "family" or the "household of God". While they experienced conflict and struggle as any family does, they knew that in the Christian fellowship they had brothers and sisters in faith who were part of a network of love and service. They were not alone.

THE NEED FOR COMMUNITY

Many people today struggle with the problem of loneliness. They feel isolated or cut off from deep relationships with other people. Within western culture, observers have noted in recent years a breakdown in the networks of "natural" community which give its members a sense of identity and of personal worth and dignity. As an increasing number of people feel this isolation, their life is drained of its warmth and sense of belonging.

In the family

There are more single parent families, and this provides us with one indicator of the changing networks of natural community. It is now common for the extended family to be spread all over the country, or the world, and in the "nuclear family" for both parents to work. In some of these families most of the available energy is focused on income production and consumption. Little may be left to give in real caring for the other members of the family.

In the neighbourhood

In addition to changes within family structures, many people experience a decline in the quality of community in the areas in which they live. Mobility decreases long-term relationships and means that we get to know our ever-changing neighbours less well. As society has shifted from a primarily rural to a primarily urban/suburban culture, some areas find that a neighbourhood may exist in name, but qualities of good neighbourliness are minimal if not non-existent. There are many places where neighbours do not even know each other's names, much less feel a sense of obligation to the well-being of the other. In some new housing developments, the first item to go up after the basic buildings are built is some type of fencing or barrier to provide privacy and distance from the neighbours who are too near. Where there are large increases in population density, people will often respond by decreasing their involvement with those around them. They do this in an attempt to compensate for having too many relationships with which to cope.

At work
Paid employment serves as a source of community for many people, particularly men. The bonds of friendship which develop during years of working together can be deep and important. Many people, however, have been made to feel less human by their jobs, in which they are treated like interchangeable pieces of machinery to be quickly discarded when the economy declines or the needs of the company change. Many feel that their employer is an enemy. Sometimes they feel a sense of competition with those working alongside them. This, along with questions about the importance and value of the work itself, can prevent the workplace from being a primary location for personal involvement and care, especially in times of distress and difficulty.

In leisure
Another factor leading towards a breakdown in community is the rise of the spectator culture, with large amounts of time given to television watching. This tends to reduce significantly the level of involvement with other people. To watch the game is very different from playing the game. The average person spends many hours watching the television. This decreases time spent in conversation, activity and personal relationships. The spectator becomes more of an observer than an active participant in life. One side-effect is that it becomes easy to criticize those who are leaders and activists in working at solving problems and meeting needs. Things look so easy until one attempts to do them oneself. Only then do the difficulties become apparent, as well as the need for sustained commitment. The deep human longing for a sense of belonging cannot be met impersonally through the media. Human beings can only be confirmed as the people God created them to be when they are involved in caring and loving personal relationships.

Through small groups
Many people do experience some community in a variety of forms throughout their day-to-day life. But many do not, and this brings a hunger for new ways to build relationships which are positive and satisfying. People today increasingly sense the bankruptcy of their situation apart from some sort of religious faith. How is that faith to be discovered and made real for the individual? When so many forces seem to pull people apart, what can bring them together? Christian small groups can be one of the answers to these most important questions.

THE CALL TO COMMUNITY
Jesus Christ calls the Church to be a fellowship of love. This is our distinctive heritage and calling. Unfortunately, all too often in a particular church the language of love may be present but the demonstration of love may be disappointing. Members may find themselves relating on only the most superficial of levels, exchanging conversation but not really sharing themselves. Institutional forms and preoccupations often give a low priority to building relationships and discourage the kind of committed fellowship which the New Testament describes and calls for.

Quality and characteristics

The New Testament speaks clearly about the character and quality of Christian community. The worksheet gives just some of the passages on this subject. They could be used as a checklist to help you think about the quality of Christian fellowship which you receive and give, and the characteristics of the church of which you are a part. Even as we acknowledge our limitations and imperfections, we are encouraged to reach towards a genuine Christian fellowship. We have the promise that what God intends he makes possible, as we give ourselves to him and to his will.

A people rather than a place

Many people today believe that their faith is an extremely personal matter, not to be discussed with anyone. The call to mutual burden-bearing, to sharing others' interests, to encouraging one another to love and good works can be heard by these people as a threat to personal dignity and freedom rather than as an invitation to a richer and more abundant life. For others, the church as an institution has become less central in the regular routine of life. This is true even for many who would consider themselves practising Christians. Recreational involvements are considered more important than participation in the activities of the Christian community. The church becomes a place to which one "goes" rather than a centre of worship and fellowship that shapes all of life. The church then tends to be seen as a "club" rather than as a "community"; as a "place" rather than as a "people".

In small groups of from three to twelve people, there is an opportunity to explore the meaning and application of Christian faith in a setting which provides a degree of security and safety. Healthy small groups can be a place where members learn how to love one another. Beyond that, good small groups provide supportive relationships which sustain Christian caring for people outside the group itself. Sustained ministry flows from supportive relationships. Costly discipleship can be nourished in a circle of care and concern. As Christians experience both the joy and the struggle involved in the Christian life, a small group drawing upon the resources of Scripture for inspiration and encouragement can experience the reality of the "koinonia" of Christ with his people.

THE BIBLE IN SMALL GROUPS

Why use the Bible in small groups?

Although small groups can meet for many purposes and draw upon many different resources, the one resource which has shaped the life of the Church more than any other throughout its long history has been the Bible. Christians have been characterized as "people of the Book" and that book has been the Bible. 2 Timothy 3.15b-17 summarizes some central aspects of the purpose and usefulness of the Bible:

> . . . you have known the Holy Scriptures, which are able to give you the wisdom that leads to salvation through faith in Christ Jesus. All Scripture is inspired by God and is useful for teaching the truth, rebuking error, correcting faults, and giving instruction for right living, so that the person who serves God may be fully qualified and equipped to do every kind of good deed.

14

Worksheet on Christian community

Present?   Instructions: Place a P, A or N next to each of the
Absent?   following verses as you consider your involvement
Need more?   in Christian community.

☐ "My commandment is this: love one another, just as I love you."
(John 15.12)

☐ Love one another warmly as Christian brothers, and be eager to show
respect for one another . . . Share your belongings with your needy
fellow-Christians, and open your homes to strangers.
(Romans 12.10, 13)

☐ Help to carry one another's burdens, and in this way you will obey the
law of Christ. (Galatians 6.2)

☐ . . . be kind and tender-hearted to one another, and forgive one
another, as God has forgiven you through Christ. (Ephesians 4.32)

☐ Don't do anything from selfish ambition or from a cheap desire to
boast, but be humble towards one another, always considering
others better than yourselves. And look out for one another's
interests, not just for your own. (Philippians 2.3-4)

☐ Be tolerant with one another and forgive one another whenever any
of you has a complaint against someone else. You must forgive one
another just as the Lord has forgiven you . . . Christ's message in all its
richness must live in your hearts. Teach and instruct one another with
all wisdom. (Colossians 3.13, 16a)

☐ Let us be concerned for one another, to help one another to show
love and to do good. Let us not give up the habit of meeting together,
as some are doing. Instead, let us encourage one another . . .
(Hebrews 10.24-25a)

☐ So then, confess your sins to one another and pray for one another,
so that you will be healed. (James 5.16a)

☐ This is how we know what love is: Christ gave his life for us. We too,
then, ought to give our lives for our brothers! . . . our love should not
be just words and talk; it must be true love, which shows itself in
action. (1 John 3.16, 18)

Pointers for life

Scripture has been written and preserved not just to give us information that shapes our thinking but to enable faith which directs our living. It tells us what we need to know about God and ourselves so that our lives can find their meaning and become satisfying and productive. Notice the aspects of life which Scripture addresses:

○ Salvation through Jesus Christ
○ Truth and error
○ Correction of faults
○ Instruction for right living
○ Equipment for doing good.

With such important topics in the Bible for the understanding and living of life, to neglect the Scriptures is to be impoverished and limited. Yet many people today are biblically illiterate. They simply do not know what the Bible says, what it means, or how to apply it to their own life. Many who have heard the Bible read in church have never opened the Bible and read it at home. Dusty unread Bibles help no one. During the Middle Ages when the Bible was available only to a few and only in Latin, the widespread ignorance of Scripture was understandable. Before and during the Reformation the work of translating the Bible into the language of the common people was considered of such importance that some, like William Tyndale and John Wycliffe, gave their lives for it.

Today we have the Scriptures translated into a number of versions, so that it can be easily understood by all. What is needed are ways to encourage and help people to open their Bibles, read them and make sense of them so that God's word in Scripture may become God's word to them day by day.

THE VALUE OF GROUP BIBLE STUDY

While sermons preached on the Bible are important to the life of a healthy congregation, and personal Bible study is valuable to those who do it, there are special benefits to be gained by small group interaction with the Scriptures. Many who do not read their Bibles at home will read them in the context of a small group. The Bible thus becomes an open book, and when good methods are used the Bible becomes a book that is understood.

Service

One result is that lay people who study the Bible together find encouragement for their lives as individuals as they work for Christ. Lay Christians are not called primarily to support the clergyman or minister in his ministry; rather the clergy are called to equip the laity for their own ministry! ". . . he [Christ] appointed some to be . . . pastors and teachers. He did this to prepare all God's people for the work of Christian service, in order to build up the body of Christ." (Ephesians 4.11b-12) All Christians have been called to be ministers or servants of Christ to accomplish his will in the world. In order to know and fulfill this call it is helpful to study the Scriptures with others who are also attempting to learn what it means to be servant Christians. Solitary servanthood is very difficult if not impossible. The interaction and discussion within a group as each individual reflects on biblical stories and themes can be very helpful to Christian growth and service.

Deeper understanding

Group interaction with the Scriptures can help individuals to broaden and deepen

16

their understanding of a given passage. It can enable people to focus and reflect upon that which, in individual study, they might have ignored or misunderstood. The comments and insights of other members of the group can correct distortions and possible misapplication of Scripture and can encourage a fuller appreciation of the biblical truth being examined.

Studies of learning reveal that while people remember approximately 10% of what they hear, they remember up to 90% of what they say. Therefore, to increase the amount of learning that occurs, increase the amount of talking about the Bible which each member does. A group discussion provides more opportunity to discuss the biblical material, which increases the likelihood of remembering what is being examined.

Increased application

Another significant benefit of using the Bible in groups is the possibility of increasing personal application of the biblical material. It can be relatively easy in much of our society to ignore the necessity of considering the relationship of biblical truth to our own lives. In a group setting where people look at the Scriptures together, it often happens almost automatically that members discuss whether the passage is relevant today and how they can apply it to their own lives. Although groups can function at a fairly high level of abstraction, usually the group setting encourages a more concrete discussion with the possibility of personal and group response to the passage being discussed. People are often helped to see how the biblical material can be related to their own lives as they hear other group members sharing how they have applied this material to themselves as appropriate circumstances have arisen. This helps members to be "doers of the word, and not hearers only" (James 1.22, RSV).

Training and resources

Some worry about the possibility that lay people using the Bible in groups may not do much more than share their ignorance. This can waste valuable time and may do spiritual harm. Groups that do not follow good methods can misuse the Bible. The appropriate remedy is not to cease using the Bible in groups but rather to provide training and resources so that the group is a healthy and productive learning experience for all involved. Groups that do not receive any training or support can at times feel alienated from the church and become inward-looking or separatist. Groups which have been provided with useful resources, training and help usually relate in a very positive way to the larger congregation. Many churches report that some of their strongest and most enthusiastic supporters and leaders have been participants in well-organized small groups.

OPPORTUNITY

These are challenging and exciting times. Needs are great. Finding and responding to spiritual hunger all around us calls for the very best that we can offer. One way of meeting such tremendous need is to help men and women hear the "Good News" of God's love. As we enable men and women to open their Bibles to hear and respond to the Word of God, we share in the privilege of changing lives for the better.

One opportunity before the Church today is to use those principles, resources, and methods which can provide practical help when people want to use the Bible in groups. Good methods heighten interest and stimulate learning and ministry. The following chapters seek to share some of the most useful things which have been learned in recent years about using the Bible in small groups. Relying upon the help of the Holy Spirit, it is hoped that those using these aids in studying the Bible may join the psalmist who prayed so long ago: "Open my eyes, so that I may see the wonderful truths in your law" (Psalm 119.18).

2

Beginning a Small Group

Once you have decided to begin a Christian small group, how do you get it started and keep it going?

Understanding some of the basic issues in group life can help you to build healthy small groups and avoid some of the more common mistakes. These issues include:

O   promise or covenant, and purpose
O   contracting
O   time
O   types of groups
O   participants
O   commitments
O   stages in group life.

PROMISE
All Christian small groups should develop a clear sense of purpose. The group members should all understand this purpose and promise to work towards achieving it. This promise is sometimes called a covenant. All human covenants find their beginnings in the covenant God made with his people. We can see God making covenants with Abraham, with the people of Israel at Sinai, in the Upper Room when Jesus introduces the "new covenant" in his blood, and many others throughout the Bible. God's covenants throughout history demonstrate the depth and intensity of his love for us. When we choose to come together in small groups, the promises we make to each other help to shape and direct our life together. They help us move from vague intention to directed commitment. Sometimes writers on small groups speak of the promises or covenants which the group members may wish to adopt. This helps us to see that coming together as Christians is more than following certain principles or using certain techniques. Group members make promises to each other and the ongoing life of the group becomes the context for promise-keeping.

What are the promises we wish to make to one another as we begin a new small group? This depends on our understanding of the purpose of coming together.

The purpose should be related to group members' commitments to the larger church congregation. The healthy small group will see itself as one part of the larger Christian community joining together to focus on particular aspects of the Christian life. At the same time it should maintain its involvement in the worship and service of the larger church.

Eight covenant dynamics

While different groups will want to adopt different promises or covenants, you may want to consider these eight suggested by Dr. Louis H. Evans Jr. as key dynamics in Christian small groups willing to make a very serious commitment to each other:

1. **The covenant of affirmation (unconditional love, agape love):** There is nothing you have done or will do that will make me stop loving you. I may not agree with your actions, but I will love you as a person and do all I can to hold you up in God's affirming love.

2. **The covenant of availability:** Anything I have – time, energy, insight, possessions – is at your disposal if you need it, to the limit of my resources. I give these to you in a priority of covenant over other non-covenant demands. As part of this availability, I pledge my time on a regular basis, whether in prayer or in an agreed-on meeting time.

3. **The covenant of prayer:** I covenant to pray for you in some regular fashion, believing that our caring Father wishes His children to pray for one another and ask Him for the blessings they need.

4. **The covenant of openness:** I promise to strive to become a more open person, disclosing my feelings, my struggles, my joys, and my hurts to you as well as I am able. The degree to which I do so implies that I cannot make it without you, that I trust you with my problems and my dreams, and that I need you. This is to affirm your worth to me as a person. In other words, I need you.

5. **The covenant of honesty:** I will try to mirror back to you what I am hearing you say and feel. If this means risking pain for either of us, I will trust our relationship enough to take that risk, realizing it is in "speaking the truth in a spirit of love" that we grow up in every way into Christ who is the head (Ephesians 4.15). I will try to express this honesty in a sensitive and controlled manner, and to meter it according to what I perceive the circumstances to be.

6. **The covenant of sensitivity:** Even as I desire to be known and understood by you, I covenant to be sensitive to you and to your needs to the best of my ability. I will try to hear you, see you, and feel where you are and to draw you out of the pit of discouragement or withdrawal.

7. **The covenant of confidentiality:** I will promise to keep whatever is shared within the confines of the group, in order to provide the atmosphere of openness.

8. **The covenant of accountability:** I consider that the gifts God has given me for the common good should be liberated for your benefit. If I should discover areas of my life that are under bondage, hung up, or truncated by my own misdoings or by the scars inflicted by others, I will seek Christ's

liberating power through His Holy Spirit and through my covenant partners so that I might give to you more of myself. I am accountable to you to become what God has designed me to be in His loving creation.

(Louis H. Evans, Jr. *Covenant to Care* Victor Books, SP Publications, P.O. Box 1825, Wheaton IL 60187)

While these particular eight covenants may not be those which your group would choose to adopt, it is helpful for every small group to think seriously about the kind of promises and expectations which underlie the group's purpose. The combination of specific "covenants" with a general statement of purpose and procedure becomes the overall "covenant" of your group.

It is good if group members have a shared understanding of the group's purpose. This will help the group to function more efficiently. Some groups might find it helpful to write down the specific promises they have made. An example is on page 22.

Shared purpose

A Christian small group can be defined as a deliberate face-to-face gathering of three to twelve people who meet regularly and share the common purpose of exploring together some aspect of Christian faith and discipleship. Within this general definition there are many different kinds of groups with differing specific purposes. Healthy small groups need a clear sense of purpose shared among the group members. A group promise is a shared understanding of the purpose of the group, with agreement on the general means that will be used to achieve that purpose. Groups experience difficulty when there is no clear sense of direction or commitment understood by all the members. The process of discussing and defining the group promise or covenant is called "contracting".

CONTRACTING

Simply to invite people to join a "Christian small group" or a "Bible study group" does not tell them clearly what they are joining and what obligations are involved. This general invitation does not adequately express what the group does or means to accomplish specifically. If you invite someone to a Bible study group, for example, it is possible that they will anticipate sitting in a class where a teacher provides information and where they are merely listeners rather than actively involved in the discussion and participating in what's going on. People can attach different meanings even to simple words. Sometimes when people hear about small groups, they assume that you are talking about a therapy group or an intensely personal group.

Common understanding

Before you invite anyone to join your small group, make sure that you know and can communicate clearly what your group will do and what is being asked of participants. Common understanding develops when sufficient time is taken to think and talk through what this particular small group is all about so that everyone understands. Defining terms is very helpful. Time taken to work on the promises that the group members make is time that allows the group organizers, and then the group itself, to focus on its reasons for meeting, and to become a more satisfying experience for all those involved.

Framework

Purpose of our group:

Our specific goals are:

The portion of the Bible that we intend to study:

Bible study method we intend to use:

Version of the Bible we plan to use:

In addition to Bible study, we would also like to:

Our leader(s) will be:

We have promised together to meet for _____ weeks, after which time we will review and evaluate our group.

We will meet each week as follows:

   Day of the week: _____

   Beginning time: _____

   Closing time: _____

Meeting place:

A typical schedule would look like this:

The ground rules that we have agreed to follow:

   Individual preparation and responsibility:

   Open group (New members welcome at any meeting and time)

   Closed group (No new members after the 3rd meeting)

   Absences:

   Meeting room:

   Food:

   Evaluation procedures:

   Time of re-evaluation:

   Visitors:

   Children:

Commitment

Studies in group dynamics reveal that people are more highly committed to groups in which they have some say about direction and functioning. Most new groups will tend to have a "contract" or statement of purpose which has been developed by the leaders who begin the group. But it is still helpful to have a discussion of this purpose at the beginning of a group, so that everyone knows what the group is about and what is expected of those who choose to participate. Allowing members to share in decisions about the length of time the group will run for, the time and place of meetings as well as the activities of the group, increases their sense of participation and belonging.

Key aspects

Key aspects of group life to be considered in contracting include:

Relationships: How will relationships among the members be built?

Scripture: How will the group use the Bible in their life together?

Prayer: What part will prayer occupy in the group?

Time: How long do we wish to meet for each time, and how many times do we wish to meet?

Intensity: What level of commitment and work do we want in the group? How hard do we want to work?

Leadership: What pattern of leadership do we want? Who is willing to take responsibility to help the group achieve its goals?

These are some of the ingredients of group life which shape the way in which a group will function and accomplish its purpose.

Re-contracting

When groups come to the end of the time period for which they initially agreed to meet, e.g. eight weeks, there is a need to "re-negotiate the contract". This means having one group meeting in which time is spent evaluating what the group has meant in the life of the members, and deciding if they wish it to continue or not. If the decision is made to continue, then the group, with its leaders, must decide what they wish to do in the weeks ahead. This process of contracting and re-contracting at periodic intervals helps to keep a group fresh and growing. Groups can lose their sense of direction yet not know what to do about it. Knowing that at least once a quarter there will be a discussion among all the group members about the promises made in the group helps to focus and deepen group life.

Questions to ask in contracting

Asking some general questions about the purpose of the group assists those considering leadership or involvement in a group to be clear about the reasons why the group is meeting. Those planning to begin a group should ask and answer these questions before they invite others to join. One or two of the questions could be asked during the first group meeting to help build a shared understanding of what the group is about. During a re-contracting discussion towards the end of a group's life cycle, these questions can help shape future group directions. Here are some examples of questions to ask when defining the purpose of the group and asking group members to promise to work towards achieving this purpose:

O   Why do we want to have a small group?

O   What do you personally want to get out of this group?
O   What goals do we want to adopt as a small group?
O   What do we want to happen in and through us as a result of our involvement in this group?
O   What ingredients do we want included in our group?
O   What don't we want to do in this group?
O   What will make this group "successful" or worth the time involved?
O   What do we want to do in our group meeting times?

TIME

How many times a group meets and the way it proportions the use of its time is determined by the purpose of the group. Most new groups benefit from setting a definite number of weeks for their initial cycle. Eight to ten weeks is common. Inviting people to join a group with a definite time limit helps to calm fears of an unending commitment. At the end of the agreed time, the group can decide to re-contract for another definite length of time, for example, three months. If some wish to leave the group at this time, they can do so with a clear conscience since their agreement was only to the initial period. This new beginning is a good point to invite new members to join.

Groups can meet at any time and place convenient for the group members. You could try:
O   weekday meetings during the day or evening
O   breakfast or luncheon meetings
O   Saturday morning meetings
O   Sunday afternoon or evening meetings.

One church has men's small groups which meet on different mornings of the week from 6.30 to 7.45 a.m. Groups for housewives meet mid-mornings during the week while children are in school. Couples' groups meet on weekday evenings. Family groups meet on Sunday afternoons. Businessmen meet for Bible study and prayer at lunch in an office or restaurant meeting room near where they work. While some groups meet regularly in an attractive room at the church, most meet in people's homes. A warm, friendly environment with flexible seating, proper lighting, fresh air and a comfortable temperature helps towards a good group meeting.

Most new groups find it advantageous to meet weekly for a time ranging from an hour and a half to two hours. Some groups, meeting for breakfast for example, may need briefer periods. But most find that about an hour and a half is necessary. Even with two hours a week of meeting time, you will need to choose what can be done. Groups that choose to meet bi-weekly or once a month will find that building personal relationships takes longer and the group will require more time to cohere. One reason why committees so seldom function as deeply meaningful Christian communities is that time is so infrequently spent together.

A common pattern for meeting is:

Arrival, conversations, light refreshments	15 minutes
Interaction with the Scriptures	30-45 minutes
Personal sharing of concerns and interests	30 minutes
Prayer	15 minutes

Keep to time

Beginning and ending the meeting on time is most important to the success of a group. When groups begin and end late, people who have other commitments will tend to reconsider their involvement in the group. A group meeting at night, for instance, which runs overtime may be very irritating to someone who has to get up early in the morning. Even if a wonderful discussion is taking place, someone should say: "It's time for us to stop now. Anyone who wants to stay around and talk is more than welcome but we need to stick to our time limit."

Different focuses
Depending upon the specific group purpose, group time will be spent in somewhat different ways. All Christian small groups emphasize the importance of relationships and communicating with each other. Groups using the Bible as a resource will naturally spend some time with the Scriptures at each meeting. Unlike most formal classes, small groups seek to provide an opportunity for all the members to talk, to share something of themselves, and to emphasize how what is being learned can be applied to daily life. The differences between groups will come in the particular focus on study, discussion or action, and in the characteristics of members.

BASIC TYPES OF SMALL GROUPS
Because there are so many different kinds of small groups, it is useful to know what type you want to have. Groups are called by many different names, and the purpose of the group and the methods used are not always obvious from the name of the group. Four basic kinds of Christian small groups which use the Bible are:
O   Study groups
O   Sharing groups
O   Ministry groups
O   Discipleship groups.

Study groups
Focus: Gaining knowledge and understanding of material, whether a book, chapter, verse in the Bible or study of a biblical character or theme.
Methods: Discovery Bible study, chapter study, book study, thematic or topical study, word studies, biographical studies.
Time: A study group will usually spend a major portion of its time on the study; perhaps forty-five minutes to an hour.

Sharing groups
Focus: Gaining insight from Scripture to apply to personal circumstances and relationships through discussion and reflection.
Methods: Sharing questions, relational Bible study, relational games, Scripture reflection exercises, etc.
Time: A substantial proportion of the time is given to personal self-disclosure and sharing how the Scriptures relate to the individual members of the group. Bible reading and reflection may take fifteen to twenty-five minutes. Personal sharing may take an hour or more.

Ministry groups
Focus: Service or action-oriented with an emphasis on applying personally and

practically what is learned from Scripture.

Kinds of ministry groups: committees, accountability groups, and mission groups.

Committees: In most churches committees are groups of people that have responsibility for making certain decisions and organizing the church's programme. Committees can function as meaningful Christian communities when they take time to care for each other as well as work together on a given task. The Bible can be used as a resource in the encouragement and instruction of the committee members.

Accountability groups: These small groups take time to discuss the ways in which each group member desires and intends to do the will of God in some specific area of life. Usually each senses a call to serve in a different place from the others. Although the forms and locations of service may differ, each is willing to share with the group how they are attempting to work out the "obedience of faith"

Mission groups: These are groups of people who sense a call to a common task and join together to try to accomplish it. They know that a group can often accomplish more than an individual. Such groups may focus on an area of need in the church or in the neighbourhood or country. Mission group members work at the common task as well as spending time in the group. Action group is another name for this kind of group.

Ministry groups may adopt daily personal Bible study and meditation as a spiritual discipline for members outside the group meeting times. This allows more of the group time to be focused on the common task.

Time: Most of the group time is focused on discussing the task, with some time given to personal sharing and Bible reflection. Task time may take ninety minutes. Sharing and prayer: thirty minutes.

Discipleship groups

These are basic Christian small groups which combine the ingredients of the other types of small groups to provide a complete experience of learning about and living the Christian faith. These are the best groups for those beginning in the faith or those with no previous group experience. Often these are called Christian growth groups or "koinonia" groups.

Focus: Discovering the possibilities to be realized in living as a Christian through personal sharing, discussion Bible study, an emphasis on active discipleship, and praying aloud.

Methods: Sharing questions, inductive discussion Bible study with attention to application, and conversational prayer.

The ingredients found in these four types of Christian small groups combine and re-combine in a wide diversity of groups existing under a large number of names. Some groups include elements not mentioned here, such as those emphasizing worship or the exercise of various spiritual gifts. Some groups spend most of their time in prayer. Others express their creativity through dance or drama, poetry or music. Family groups bring together children and adults in intergenerational experiences. The possibilities for group life are as varied as people are. Most churches who are beginning small groups for the first time, however, will find that encouraging discipleship groups provides a good foundation from which other kinds of small groups can develop and grow.

PARTICIPANTS

Who should be invited to join your small group? How will you discover who might be interested?

Small groups grow and flourish when they are made up of people who have been personally invited to join. Impersonal invitations, such as announcements in a church bulletin or newsletter, inform people about the existence of a new group but usually do not result in lots of volunteers wanting to become involved.

The first step in beginning a group, after thinking through a general statement of purpose and what the group will do, is to pray about possible participants. Next recruit one or two people to share in the organization and planning of the group. Groups seem to thrive on shared leadership. After two or three people are committed to beginning a group, then the challenge comes to find three to nine others. If each person invites three or four others to consider being involved, the necessary minimum to begin will probably respond.

Who to ask

Throw the net wide. Do not decide in advance who will and will not be interested. Talk about the new group with as many different people as possible. See who is interested. One woman who considered beginning a neighbourhood Bible study believed that no one in her neighbourhood would be interested. She decided to take two weeks and attempt to visit each of her neighbours, telling them about the group and asking if they might consider it. In eleven conversations there were eleven women who expressed interest! From outside it is difficult to know where a person is spiritually. Give people an opportunity to make their own decision about involvement. Do not decide for them by refusing to invite them.

Consider diversity and homogeneity in the group. It helps if a group has members who are somewhat different from each other in personality and backgrounds yet who share a common interest in the purposes of the group. Whether groups are all male, all female or mixed will depend on the purpose and timing of the group. There are values in each type. People in groups composed of one sex only often experience a freedom and honesty that is more difficult in mixed groups. Mixed groups accomplish some things not possible in a same-sex group. Marriages, for instance, are sometimes strengthened in couples' groups because the sharing of common experiences and problems can give couples greater perspective and understanding.

When you do not know who to invite, ask your minister or leaders in your congregation for names of those who might be interested. Ask your friends for names. Consider inviting acquaintances or neighbours who do not go to church. Pray and ask God to send those who should participate. Sometimes it may take three months before a new group can begin with a full complement of eight to twelve members. Consider beginning when you have four or five, and increase the size of the group as time goes along.

How to ask

When inviting people to consider involvement in a new group, the right language and attitude is very important. Attempt to express why you yourself are involved in this group and what you expect the group to do. Convey a sense of positive excitement. Expect the person to whom you are talking to be responsive. Don't be like the poor salesman who begins every conversation with a prospective customer by saying: "I know you don't want this but let me tell you about it anyway." Choose words and phrases which will be understood and will not frighten away an uncertain beginner.

Introductory meeting

A good way to invite people who are uncertain about whether or not they want to be involved is to have an introductory meeting. People can be invited to an informal gathering with refreshments and a sample abbreviated small group experience. No commitment to ongoing involvement is required of those coming to this information meeting. Since some of those invited may not decide to continue, it helps to invite a few more than the desired final number of group members. Plan this information meeting carefully so that it is non-threatening, positive and helpful to people making a decision about the future.

COMMITMENTS

Once a decision has been made about what kind of group you want and who you want to invite, it is time to consider what commitments need to be made by the group members. Commitments are the disciplines and norms which the group is willing to adopt in order to accomplish its purpose. Disciplines are the guidelines within which group members agree to function. Norms are shared expectations about appropriate behaviour within the group.

Generally speaking there are at least three basic commitments necessary to the health and growth of any Christian small group. These are regular attendance, confidentiality, and strictly limited advice-giving.

Attendance

Although some groups choose to be casually structured and open to whoever shows up at a particular meeting, most groups discover that a commitment to regular attendance is absolutely essential.

Sometimes people will say that they want to be in a small group but they have conflicting obligations which will require them to miss some of the meetings. This may be acceptable in some circumstances. Yet if the purpose of the group includes building relationships of love and care among the members, a floating population will make it difficult, if not impossible, to accomplish the group's purpose. Hard as it may be, those choosing to be in a group may have to alter or postpone, for the time being, some of their other commitments. When people share together in discussion and prayer, a level of trust is built up week by week. When some are absent or casual about their attendance, that building of trust is delayed or denied. Those for whom the group is a high priority may come to resent or shut out the less frequent attenders. Relationships need time and trust to develop. Those invited to join a group should be asked to commit themselves to attend each meeting until the end of the contract period.

The one kind of group which would probably not emphasize the importance of regular attendance is a neighbourhood Bible study or out-reach group seeking to share the gospel with non-Christian or non-churchgoing friends and neighbours. Such a group may function as an open fellowship group welcoming any who come each week. Even in this kind of group, unless there is a core of people who come regularly, the group will not usually last very long.

Confidentiality

The second basic commitment necessary to a healthy small group is adopting the discipline of confidentiality.

This discipline assumes that anything that is shared in the group will not be mentioned outside it, even to close friends or spouses. The only exception would be if permission were explicitly given by the person sharing. Breaking confidentiality destroys trust. Only very safe and public things will be discussed in a group where there is no assurance of confidentiality. This is why privacy must be protected. If someone believes that what they share in the group will be spread all over the church or in the neighbourhood, they will wisely limit their remarks. This will impede the ability of the group to function as a true Christian community, helping "to carry one another's burdens" so as to fulfil the law of Christ (Galatians 6.2).

Advice-giving

The third basic commitment in healthy small groups is to agree strictly to limit the amount of advice-giving done in the group. One common tendency when someone shares a concern or problem is for other group members to begin telling the speaker what he or she ought to do. Often these solutions are proposed long before the true situation has been really understood. Careful listening should precede any suggestions. James tells us to be "quick to listen, but slow to speak" (James 1.19). Advice which is given quickly may do more harm than good. It is more helpful to listen carefully and ask questions which help the speaker to clarify for himself what the problem is. In this way he may be able to decide what he thinks he should do in the situation. Even people who ask for advice usually resist it when given.

Other commitments

Additional commitments which the group might adopt depend upon the specific goals of the group. Many groups adopt disciplines of prayer and Bible reading as part of their commitment. Some stress attendance at worship. Others take on financial commitments to a needy project or person. Others adopt disciplines relevant to their mission. It is important that the commitments the group chooses to adopt are realistic and honest. Sometimes groups set themselves impossible goals and this can lead to guilty feelings and false relationships.

One example is a group which agrees that everyone will study their Bible daily during the week. Sometimes the leader will tell the group that they should do this and no one risks saying that he will find it difficult. Very few members of small groups actually do homework during the week. Simply announcing that people should doesn't mean that they will! Another example is someone in a group saying, "Let's all pray for each other every day between meetings." This is a worthy discipline, but unless the group members are really committed to it, it will result in failure, guilt and frustration. When someone wishes to suggest a new discipline for the group, make sure that it is discussed and agreed to seriously. Sometimes it may be necessary to say that the group wants to encourage a particular discipline without saying that it is a definite commitment expected of all the group members.

Decisions must also be made about when and where to meet, the duties of the leaders and members, the bringing of Bibles and/or study materials, the handling of refreshments and, where applicable, deciding how the children will be looked after. Chapter 3 will discuss leadership patterns.

Bibles

In a group using the Bible it is important that each person has a copy of the Bible, preferably all the same version. Sometimes groups have purchased or borrowed inexpensive Bibles so that all may have one version in common even if they use other versions for comparison and in personal study. In couples' groups it is important that both the husband and wife have a copy of the Bible. Otherwise one may be less involved in the group discussion.

Refreshments

Refreshments can help or hinder a group. If they are too elaborate or too time-consuming, they can interfere with the group's purpose. Having refreshments at the end of the meeting which require the host or hostess to leave before the conclusion limits his or her involvement in the group. Simple, inexpensive refreshments can make people feel more at home and help them to enjoy the time together.

It is often good to arrange for the meeting to be held in the home of a person other than the leader who will lead the study. The host can be responsible for refreshments and welcoming those coming, while the discussion leader can focus on the content and process of the meeting. Shared leadership lightens the load on each one and encourages a sense that the group belongs to all its members, not just to a single designated leader.

Child care

If group members have children, then arrangements need to be made for them. Sensitivity needs to be shown here, especially towards young mothers who are often expected to care for children rather than participate fully in the group without fear of distraction. Unless the group is a family group designed to include children in its activities, arrangements should be made for children to be cared for away from the group meeting room. A baby-sitter can be arranged or couples can take turns being responsible for the children. It might be that the cost of a baby-sitter could be shared by the whole group.

Norms

Norms or shared expectations about appropriate behaviour in a group are usually considered "obvious", needing little or no discussion. Some common norms in group life include:
O   a willingness to listen to group members and not dominate the discussion
O   a willingness to talk and not sit silent for the entire meeting
O   an intention to take the Scriptures seriously as worthy of study and thought
O   an openness to the other members' ideas and opinions
O   a desire to know and be known by the other group members.

A very important norm in healthy small groups concerns the place of feelings in the group. Human beings think; they also feel. Bible-oriented groups will include some Bible study in each group meeting. But at every meeting there will also be the feelings and experiences present in each group member. The small group provides a context for the appropriate sharing of feelings, both positive and negative, as group members desire. Both the head and the heart come to group meetings. The expression of feelings builds understanding and trust when people respond positively.

Occasionally members of the group experience conflict. This, too, is normal and natural. People are different and these differences affect their behaviour in the group. People function on different levels of intensity. They care about different things. They have different spiritual gifts. Some of the best learning will occur as members practise "speaking the truth in a spirit of love" (Ephesians 4.15) and work through conflict rather than denying or repressing it. While the expression of feelings should not dominate the group's time, neither should such expression be denied, criticized or unduly limited. Sensitivity and wisdom should guide group sharing and response. If the need being expressed is unusually pressing, an attempt should be made to help the person obtain assistance from someone known to the group who is capable of giving such help, possibly a clergyman or counsellor. Groups should acknowledge their limitations and know when and where to go for help.

STAGES IN GROUP LIFE
Small groups go through stages as they begin, continue and end their life together. Just as an individual moves through stages in his life from infancy to old age, so groups, too, move through cycles. Each group moves through its group cycle in a slightly different way depending on the experience, personalities and backgrounds of the members. There are a number of ways to describe these stages. Here is one way:

1. Pre-contract stage
The pre-contract is what you say to each other and mutually agree upon before the first "official" meeting of the group. This is where a group begins. One person or more has an idea about beginning a small group. Having got permission from the church they think about the purpose of the group and who might participate. They make preliminary decisions about how to get started and then invite others to join on the basis of this preliminary understanding. Groups that begin without this stage struggle in the next stage to reach agreement. Groups that form around a pre-contract tend to move quickly through the next few stages.

If you gather a group of people together with no more definition than "let's start a small group," much time will have to be spent defining terms and finding a sense of direction and activities that everyone can agree on. Often this will mean compromising a purpose which may be very important to one or more of the group members in order to keep everyone involved. Groups formed in this way tend to settle for the lowest common denominator as the group's purpose, and avoid activities which would stretch or threaten any members.

Consider, for example, inviting people to ". . . join a discipleship group to meet for eight weeks. We will spend some time each week discussing the Bible, getting to know each other and learning how to pray together so that we can grow in our Christian faith." Being as specific as this allows people who are not interested to decline the invitation to join the group before attending the first meeting.

2. Orientation stage
When a group first meets, each member tends to experience conflicting feelings

of attraction and repulsion. While having chosen to be there, they are still testing the group to see if it can be a satisfying and worthwhile experience for them. Each wonders whether or not he will be accepted.

Good leadership will work to help people feel comfortable during this stage while they are getting acquainted with each other and with the group process. Members in this stage may feel unsure, dependent, and hesitant about their participation until something is done which helps them to feel included and important. Patterns of participation are set during this orientation period. If someone remains silent through the entire first meeting, they are likely to remain silent throughout most of the group cycle. If they talk a lot the first night, they are likely to continue talking a lot in future meetings. Comfortable seating arrangements, good communication patterns and a good leader who encourages people to participate can help a group to settle down sooner than if no planning is done or no direction given. Some discussion of the group's promise or covenant should take place in this stage.

3. Power and control stage
This stage may begin early in the first meeting as members seek to determine the group's purpose and the promises the group will make, and find their own roles within the group. Issues of influence and control emerge, sometimes very subtly. If there is no designated leader, questions of leadership can dominate the group agenda. If there is a designated leader, someone in the group might wish to challenge either the leader or the suggested procedures for the group, and this will take time to resolve. While sometimes visible and clear, more often this stage is subtle, and many members may not be very conscious of it. There are likely to be issues of silence and talkativeness, or dominance and deference present. Group members work out ways of handling disagreements and conflicting opinions. The discovery of freedom and limits and what is appropriate behaviour in this group are being worked at even as the group carries on its stated agenda.

Most groups work through the obvious issues of power and control in the first or second meeting. When a group does not resolve these issues, it may never become very satisfying. One problem at this stage is the danger of settling down to a permanent pattern of authoritarian leadership and a passive membership (see pages 40 to 45). Working out how involvement in the group will be shared and equalized is critical to the successful resolution of this stage.

4. Trust stage
This is the stage when a group begins to feel a sense of belonging and unity. Attitudes shift from thinking primarily about what do "I" want out of this group to what do "we" want. The level of emotional involvement deepens and people begin to speak of "our group" or "the group". Members sense a giving and receiving of affection. Usually there is more laughter, more enjoyment and celebration in the group time. While conflict may be experienced, members sense a mutual commitment to solve problems and maintain good relationships.

Although a new group may have very positive experiences during the first few meetings, it still takes time for trust to develop. Evidences of trust include the amount and depth of personal self-disclosure and the way in which the group approaches its study or task. During earlier stages, for example in a Bible study, members may display their Bible knowledge or hide their ignorance because they are concerned about how the other members will react. As trust develops, a more open and honest interaction with the Scriptures becomes typical. Questions long thought about, but never asked, may be brought into the open. Members cease trying to impress each other and begin listening more carefully. Personal needs and concerns may be shared rather than hidden or denied. Negative and positive feelings emerge in the safety of a sense of acceptance and belonging. The level of conversation moves from the casual and the cliché to the personal and caring.

Many groups discover that the full move into the trust stage takes at least three, four or five weeks to happen. This is one reason to stress a commitment to attend all the meetings of a new small group. It may be too soon to make a decision about continued participation after one or two meetings, as it is difficult to assess what will really happen in a group. Groups need time to "jell". Leaders and members need to be patient in their expectations.

During the trust stage the group may move from dependence on the leader through a reactive stage of independence and testing of trust. If the leader allows the group to explore and grow, the group can move to a new and deeper level of interdependence. As time passes, people increasingly value each other and their time together. Groups may stay in the trust stage from several months to several years with some "ups and downs".

5. Differentiation or change stage

After groups have been together for a while and a sense of trust and belonging has developed, they may plateau and stay in this stage for a long time or they may experience differentiation or change. At this point group members begin to sense a need to change either their own roles in the group or the work of the group as a whole or both. Sometimes this becomes evident where there is a challenge to the patterns which have felt satisfying up to now. At times it is reflected in a desire to change leaders or change the group's purpose and the promises made. This is a sign of success in a group, because when this comes after the trust stage it demonstrates that growth is occurring.

Occasionally a few members of the group may become dissatisfied while others remain contented. A group which has felt positive and productive may begin to feel stagnant or boring. A leader may want someone else to lead. A quiet member may become much more assertive. A serious member may want some time for relaxation. A clowning member may want to become serious. People may sense that they have come to like each other too much to risk being honest in their ongoing relationships. They wonder: "Where do we go from here?"

When these feelings become obvious, it is important that group members discuss what is happening without blaming each other for the change that is occurring. Growth is good even if it is uncomfortable. Handling it requires a re-assessment of the group's purpose and ways of working. People function at different levels of growth and it may be that this particular group can no longer meet the needs of all the members.

If challenged, a leader may experience pressure and a sense of frustration when group members want something new or different. Yet the movement of the group from dependence upon its initial leaders to interdependence with group members taking more responsibility for decisions, is a normal and healthy one. A wise leader will rejoice at the growth that is taking place even if it raises difficult questions.

The appropriate response to differentiation is to take group time for evaluation and re-negotiating the contract. Practising good communication skills, such as active listening and clarification, are very helpful here as in other aspects of group life.

6. Conclusion or new beginning

After a group has an evaluation discussion, it needs to make a decision about whether or not to continue. If the time has come for the group to end, this should be accepted gracefully. Members may need to move on to other commitments. Spend some time at the last meeting sharing: "One thing I have learned in this group is . . ." or "One thing I have appreciated about this group is . . ." If a definite length of time for the duration of the group was set as part of the initial covenant, ending the group, while sad, is not traumatic. If no ending time was set, people may feel hurt that some do not wish to continue or that the group is ending. Inevitably, there is grief involved when a positive group experience must end. One way to help with this is to plan a party for the group's last meeting. Celebrate together the good things which have happened and commit each other to the Lord for the future. Or plan to have a group reunion for dinner or an outing in about three months so as to soften the pain of separation. Do not, however, keep a group going just to prevent hurting someone's feelings. See this ending as the beginning of new opportunities.

If all or many of the group members decide to continue, decisions must be made about the promises, and commitments of the ongoing group need clarification. Sufficient discussion time should be taken to work through key issues. Sometimes new members need to be invited to join in order to strengthen and bring freshness to the group. When new members join, care should be taken to include them fully in the group discussion and activity. Otherwise they may feel excluded or ignored even if ongoing members did not intend this. In many ways, this is a new beginning even if not a totally new group.

Most small groups last for about two years if they decide to continue after the initial eight to ten weeks. A few groups will re-contract year after year. I know of more than one church that has small groups which have met for over twenty years. Such long-term groups can become stale and lose a clear sense of purpose, but with periodic re-assessment, they can be deep experiences of true Christian community.

SUMMARY

Although there are many things to consider when planning to begin a new small group, actually starting is not difficult. **When the desire is there, a way will be found.** Most groups begin when one friend asks another to consider being involved in a small group. No high degree of expertise is required to make a good start. A willingness to venture, trusting God to lead and help, is the first step. On page 35 is a summary of the other steps to begin a small group.

Steps to begin a small group

Get ready!

1. Determine your purpose. What do you want to accomplish in this small group experience? What needs do you want to meet? What results do you hope for? What do you want to do? Pray.

2. Recruit one or two partners. Discuss with them your ideas for a small group. Ask them if they would like to be involved.

3. Discuss your idea with the appropriate leaders in your church. Ask for suggestions and consider possible resources and materials.

4. Pray and plan together. Re-define your purpose. Think about possible participants. Search for resources to help you accomplish your purpose. Decide on timing. — How long will each meeting be? How many weeks will the group meet?

5. Decide on a time and place for the first meeting. Set the date several weeks in advance to give people time to plan.

Make contacts!

6. Invite people to join the group. Invite more people than you want in the group so that you will have a good size even if some turn you down. Share the purpose of the group as you invite people. Be honest; be positive.

7. Determine your leadership pattern. Will one person lead the meeting each week? Will different people lead different parts of the meeting under the direction of an overall co-ordinator? Or will a different person lead each week?

8. Choose resources or the methods you will use. What section of Scripture will you study? How will you approach it? Will you use a printed guide? Will everyone have copies?

Meet together!

9. Plan and conduct your first meeting. Emphasize building relationships and discussing the purpose of the group and the length of the contract period.

10. Evaluate the first meeting and decide on future directions. Pray for those who came. Contact any who did not arrive who were expected. Encourage each other. Plan next week's meeting. Ask others to help as needed.

11. Plan to have a group discussion about how the group is going about the fifth week or so. Prepare to discuss whether the group wishes to continue on to the end of the contract period. Have suggestions about what the group might do if it continues, so that a good choice can be made by the group.

3

Leadership and Membership in the Small Group

Who can lead a small group, and what are the tasks and styles of leadership?

The small group leader is not a teacher, and the small group is not a traditional class sitting in rows of chairs listening to a lecture. Learning comes through interaction and discovery, and a good group helps people to experience the joy of discovery as they read and discuss.

Who can lead?

The small group leader should be willing to help the people in the group to have the best possible experience of discovery as they study the Bible for themselves. It is not necessary to be an expert on the Bible, or to know all about group dynamics. Sometimes people hesitate to lead because of their lack of experience or background. Many people, however, who have very little formal training make good group leaders.

In addition to Christian faith, the most important requirement for being a good group leader is a willingness to be a responsible servant of the group in order to help it accomplish its goals. This means that while a leader does not need to know the answers to all possible questions, a leader must be willing to guide the group in an orderly process of discovery and discussion. Small group leaders are often called **facilitators** or **enablers**, to stress their role as helpers and guides rather than as teachers or experts. The group "facilitator" cares about helping each member of the group to become positively involved with the biblical text and with the other members of the group.

A successful group requires at least one person who is willing to do more than ask "What's in this for me?" A good leader should be concerned about the growth and development of the group as a whole, and seek to help the members of the group accomplish their purpose. A positive Christian faith, a liking for people, a servant spirit, and a desire to explore the meaning of Scripture with others are more important qualities than sophisticated techniques. It is helpful if the person leading a group has had some previous experience as a participant in a good small group. Even if no such group or training experience is available,

36

many groups have prospered with committed, although inexperienced, leadership.

TASKS OF LEADERSHIP

The tasks of leadership are basically simple. As you lead, be ready to:
○ Pray
○ Prepare
○ Guide
○ Care.

Task 1: Pray

Prayer deepens and strengthens both the group leader and the members of the group. It is important that we pray for:

1. Wisdom as decisions are made about the group and about the particular study or activities of the group.

2. The leader's own life and role in the group.

3. Each member of the group by name and for the group as a whole, both between meetings as well as during meetings.

Because a basic purpose of the group is spiritual growth, a reliance upon the Holy Spirit as demonstrated through prayer is essential. Further, when group members are prayed for by name during the week, the leader gains a heightened sensitivity to each one and to the work of God in each life.

Task 2: Prepare

There are three major elements of preparation for a group meeting:

1. Preparing the location, setting and resources which the group will use. This involves checking the meeting place and the seating provided, and arranging for any printed or audio-visual resources that will be needed during the meeting. Hold the meeting in a comfortable environment, with the seating arranged so that all can easily see and talk with each other. This usually means arranging the chairs in a circle. The lighting needs to be good enough to read the text, and the room needs proper ventilation so it does not become too warm.

Anticipate needs and problems which may arise and take steps to solve them so that unnecessary group time will not be wasted. Make sure there are extra copies of the Bible available for any who need them, or copies of the study guide being used. Thinking ahead can help the session to flow smoothly with minimum interruptions.

2. Preparing for the meeting itself.
○ How will the meeting begin and end?
○ What will happen at the meeting apart from Bible study?
○ Will people be asked to share or to pray? If so, it would be useful to think about ways of building relationships and finding or developing a "sharing question" to aid in this.
○ How should time be apportioned for the various activities of the meeting?
○ Will reports on the week's activities be given by one or more members?
○ How can adequate time be made available for interaction with Scripture?

The prepared leader will think through the way in which time should be used, and will have a plan for how to move from one element to another. *Others may be asked to help with one aspect or another of the meeting time.*

3. **Preparing for the interaction with Scripture.** This is the most demanding of the tasks, and it usually involves the leader spending time working on the text which the group will study when it comes together. After personal study, the leader must make decisions about the questions to be asked and the procedures to be followed during the group meeting. If the group is using pre-prepared study materials, the leader may need to decide which questions to omit or which to add in at the meeting.

In many ways a group leader or facilitator is like a tour guide with a group of travellers on a journey of exploration. It helps a lot if the guide has at least seen the territory before he shows others over it. A good guide has studied the terrain with enough care so that although he may not know everything, he can at least tell people where to look to see the most important highlights.

A good Bible study leader carefully prepares before the meeting. Often this step of preparation is concluded when the leader writes down on a card or single sheet of paper the questions which will be asked or the procedures which will be followed during the group time. This card or sheet of paper can be placed in the leader's Bible and be used unobtrusively during the meeting.

At the end of this chapter you will find a worksheet designed to help the leader prepare for the meeting.

Task 3: Guide

During the meeting the leader should help the group to move through its activities on time and in an ordered way. If various parts of the meeting have been assigned to other group members, e.g. if someone has been asked to lead the discussion besides the usual group leader or facilitator, the leader will still want to help whenever needed to keep the group moving along in its work. Otherwise the group may get bogged down, spend too much time on trivial issues, or stay too long in unproductive debate or controversy.

Key aspects of the guiding task include:

O   Beginning and ending the group on time.
O   Making sure each person can see everyone else easily.
O   Asking good questions in a logical order.

O   Keeping the discussion moving at a lively pace.
O   Pulling the group back to the main subjects and away from tangents or unprofitable debate.
O   Involving as many members as possible in the discussion.
O   Keeping a check on the time so that each activity is given enough time.

While each of these aspects is important, probably the most vital is asking good questions. Good questions are:

O   Clear.
O   Focused on one main idea or thought at a time.
O   Needing more than "yes" or "no" as an answer.
O   Clearly based on the text.
O   Conversational in tone rather than stilted or formal.
O   Interesting.
O   Not too complex.
O   Open-ended, allowing for more than one response.

In asking questions, the leader should:

38

○ Not be afraid of silence, thus giving people time to think.
○ Not criticize an answer but ask "What do others think?"
○ Focus the answers by asking "Where do you see that in the text?"
○ Broaden the discussion by asking "Does anyone have anything to add?"
○ Use only questions that have not already been answered in the previous discussion.
○ Not answer his own questions, but after others have spoken, feel free to participate in the general discussion.

Ada Lum, in a helpful introduction to a Bible study guide (*Jesus the Disciple Maker*, InterVarsity Press, 1974, page 11) says this of the leader's task:

> The designated leader initiates the study discussion and guides only enough so that members themselves can discover what God has said in the passage. This does not mean that he does less preparation but probably more! Only if he is thoroughly familiar with the passage, and with the points he wants to help people find, will he be free from his question sheet and sensitive to the group and the flow of the discussion. The prepared questions only guide and suggest. As he listens, he will naturally use spontaneous questions. Furthermore, his flexibility should encourage freedom of expression and interacting questions from the group.

Task 4: Care

During and between meetings, a good leader should demonstrate a concern for the well-being of each of the group members. This is done through careful observation and listening to each of the group members in order to discern individual needs, which may be either spoken or unspoken.

Sometimes comments are made which discourage or criticize. The thoughtful leader can balance these with a word of encouragement or affirmation.

Occasionally a member is ignored or disregarded. The leader can ask an easy question addressed by name to the silent one and let him or her know that their contribution is valued.

At times a member might express an opinion which others in the group attack. The leader can protect the right of each to speak and the need of all to listen.

Sometimes a group member is experiencing great personal difficulty or loss. The leader can help that one to share the need and suggest to the group how to pray and help.

The sensitive leader can model a way of listening and responding which helps each group member to become more caring than they might be without the leader's example. Although the task of caring for each other belongs to all the members of the group, a thoughtful and empathetic leader can set a tone which will help the group grow in its ability to listen to each other and care for each other as they search the Scriptures together.

A group member may experience difficulties so great that the help which the group members or leader can give is not adequate. Deep emotional problems can be beyond the ability and experience of the group to handle. While Christian small groups can be therapeutic, they are not set up to be therapy groups. When personal needs are intense, when suffering is severe, when deep depression or suicidal inclinations appear, it is critical that the group leader meets the person outside of the group meeting and tries to assist the distressed member in obtaining appropriate help. Groups can do some things but they cannot do all things. A wise leader knows his or her limitations and goes for help when it is needed. This shows care and concern.

Leaders may be male or female depending upon the composition, purpose and traditions of the group. Many couples' groups have a husband and wife team as the co-leaders who take turns performing various functions in the group. Because small Bible study groups are not teaching groups, status or distinction is less important in a leader than an ability and willingness to perform the needed tasks of leadership. Sometimes the decision about leadership is best made by discovering who is able and willing to pray, prepare, guide and care. This may not always be the "obvious" or most talkative member or most knowledgeable member of the group.

STYLES OF LEADERSHIP

Students of small groups have discovered that there are various styles of group leadership, some of which are more helpful than others. The four most common are:

O   Autocratic
O   Authoritative
O   Democratic
O   Laissez-faire.

The accompanying chart lists some of the characteristics of each style.

In most Christian small groups beginning with new leaders or with new participants unfamiliar with how groups function, it has been found that a strong leader, who is not autocratic or totally domineering, may be more helpful than one who leaves all the decisions to the group members right from the very beginning. A well-prepared leader with a clear idea of where he or she wants to go, who is open to discussion and the active involvement of the group members, may give the inexperienced group members a sense of direction and security which is helpful in the early stages of group life. If this **authoritative** leader does not use his strength, however, to involve the group members in shared communication and decision-making practices as the weeks go by, then the group may become excessively dependent and unable to develop as it should.

Autocratic or domineering leaders smother the ideas and opinions of the group members, who may become resentful, hostile and frustrated at their lack of influence within the group. **Laissez-faire** or passive leaders may allow the group to drift with very little guidance. In such a group, a talkative member may monopolize the time or discussions may wander without moving forward.

The best leadership styles seem to be those in which prepared leaders offer suggestions and guidance most strongly in the beginning (**authoritative**) and move as rapidly as possible to a truly shared ownership of the group by all its members (**democratic**). By the end of the first agreed number of meetings, the group members should be exercising many of the functions in the group and sharing as equal partners in decision-making about future plans and procedures.

PATTERNS OF LEADERSHIP

There are a variety of patterns of leadership which a group may wish to consider as it thinks about how to conduct its meetings. These are:

O   **One leader for every session.** This is the most common pattern, when one person directs the activities of the group during its meeting for an agreed number

40

Leadership Style

	Autocratic (Domineering, dictatorial)	Authoritative (Definite yet responsive)	Democratic (Group-centered)	Laissez-faire (Permissive, passive)
	1. Total control, with members as listeners and followers.	1. Strong control, with members actively involved in the discussions.	1. Shared control, with leader and members sharing functions.	1. Minimal control, with members directing.
	2. Determines goals and policies.	2. Has a definite purpose and plan but is open to modification.	2. Shares leadership responsibility.	2. Doesn't prepare and lets things drift.
	3. More interested in subject matter (content) than people (process).	3. Active and energetic and seeks the activity of others.	3. Believes in other people.	3. Doesn't seem to care.
	4. Makes decisions regardless of other views.	4. Prepared to give direction and support as needed.	4. Creates a sense of security and belonging.	4. Causes the group to accomplish very little.
	5. Talks too much.	5. Uses communication skills to involve others.	5. Ensures that others have chance to lead.	5. Encourages fragmentation through indiscipline.
	6. Focuses attention on himself or herself.	6. Takes responsibility until others can assume it.	6. If leader withdraws, group will not fall apart.	6. Makes no attempt to appraise or regulate events.
	7. Group members are almost puppets.	7. Uses personal power to empower others.	7. Sees that group discusses all policies.	7. Lacks courage in making decisive plans.
In a Bible study:	8. Asks and answers all questions.	8. Prepares and asks questions; members respond.	8. May ask other(s) to lead discussion, using guide.	8. Asks one vague or general question, then is silent.

(Source: Items 1 and 8 in each column, and all the items in the "Authoritative" column, are by the author. The other items are from John Mallison, *Building Small Groups in the Christian Community*, Renewal Publications, Australia, 1978)

of meetings, e.g. eight to ten weeks. At the end of this time, the group may wish to select another leader or continue with the same one. The advantage of having the same leader each week is continuity, a familiar pattern, and the likelihood of development in the depth of the group as the weeks go by because members feel secure knowing how the leader will run the group.

O   **Partnership pattern leadership.** In this method, two or three people are designated as the group leaders and they share the various tasks of leadership week by week. One member may lead one week and another person the next time. Or one member may lead one part of the meeting and another lead a different part. Sometimes one person or a couple, for example, acts as the host for the evening, providing refreshments, welcoming people and building relationships while another acts as the discussion leader.

O   **Rotating leadership.** In this pattern, each member takes a turn at leading. The advantage is that no one person is burdened with preparation for all of the group meetings and all have an opportunity to learn by leading. The maximum number of members is involved. If adequate guidance is not given, however, the disadvantage may be that some will not be clear about what leading a group really involves and may be less able to help the group have a good discussion or stay on track.

The sort of leadership pattern that each group chooses will be determined by the willingness of members to serve, the amount of time available for preparation, the quality and kinds of resources available, and the specific purpose of the group. There is no such thing as a leaderless group, however. If a group does not decide on a leadership pattern suitable for its situation and circumstances, it cannot expect to function productively. Churches beginning small groups need to select and train leaders as one of the first and most important parts of building a small group programme. Leadership is too important to be left to chance. Good leaders make for good groups.

MEMBERSHIP FUNCTIONS IN THE SMALL GROUP

What are the responsibilities of the members of the small group?

While leadership is important, healthy groups have members who make significant contributions to the group. The group does not "belong" to the leader; it "belongs" to all the members. When asked, "Whose group is this?" a healthy group answers, "This is *our* group." The quality, caring and depth of a small group is the responsibility of all the members of the group.

Groups are not productive if members are passive. All members must be active, willing to use their energies, to be involved, to discuss, to listen, to care, to participate. A few members who just "sit there" can be deadly to a group. The silent member who never contributes can depress and inhibit other group members. The over-talkative or argumentative member can overwhelm the less assertive.

Only when each member makes a positive contribution does the group begin to achieve its potential. Each and every group member has an important contribution to make.

What should a good group member be willing to do?

Responsibilities of a group member

Each member should:

○ Desire the will of God for themselves and for the group.

○ Listen carefully, seeking to understand other group members.

○ Speak regularly, without sitting totally silent and without dominating the other members of the group.

○ Refrain from attacking and criticizing other members.

○ Bring a positive desire for personal and group growth.

○ Express an interest in other members' needs, concerns, and ideas, and not just seek the opportunity to express their own.

○ Express honestly their own ideas, opinions, and questions.

○ Study the passage carefully and interact with other people's ideas.

○ Question others to gain more information and different viewpoints.

Member functions

In addition to these general responsibilities of group members, there are specific functions which members may perform in the small group. These functions can be divided into two main types:

1. Those which help the group accomplish its task, such as study or action.

2. Those which help the group members build relationships or help the group's maintenance needs.

Task functions:

○ Information- and opinion-giving

This is what I know and/or believe, think, or feel.

○ Information- and opinion-seeking

What do you know, believe, think or feel?

○ Direction- and role-definer

Where are we going and what will each of us do to get there?

○ Summarizer

This is what we have said, discussed and/or decided.

○ Energizer

I'm ready to work and find this worthwhile. How about you?

○ Comprehension checker

Do we all understand what we have decided? Do we need to clarify? Is anything unclear? . . . Did you understand what Colin meant? Colin, is this what you meant . . . ?

Relationship or maintenance functions:

○ Encourager of participation

Susan, what do you think of . . . ? I'd like to hear what John has to say . . . Ralph, do you agree or disagree with . . . ?

○ Communication facilitator

Asking questions; using clarifying or paraphrasing skills.

○ Tension reliever

Using humour or telling a story to diffuse intensity or conflict.

○ Process observer

Noting who is performing which functions in the group and reporting it to the group; leading a discussion on communication in the group; noting patterns of interaction and silence; noting how time is used.

O Supporter and affirmer

Speaking positively about a member's participation in the group; affirming something that has been said or suggested.

O Interpersonal problem-solver

Helping members in conflict to listen carefully to each other; finding areas of agreement as well as areas of disagreement; identifying the unity present without ignoring differences; positive acknowledgment of conflict without hostility.

Non-helpful functions:

There are also some functions which can be seen as unhelpful.

O Blocker

A person who accepts no suggestions and rejects all efforts at compromise; usually disagrees; withholds help.

O Antagonist

A person who repeatedly criticizes or attacks one or more members of the group, always disagreeing with their ideas or suggestions; deflates others' status; defends or asserts self.

O Joker

A person who uses humour to divert the group from its purpose and to keep the group from serious and thoughtful discussion.

O Troubled

A person in such emotional distress that every question or comment is taken very personally; dominates group with own problems and is unable to listen to or care for others; over-reacts to feelings expressed in group.

Each group member performs one or more functions within the group. Often groups will have two kinds of members within it—those more oriented to the task, and those more oriented to relationships. Both dimensions are integral to a group's healthy functioning.

GETTING THE MOST FROM A GROUP

When a caring leader is well prepared,
and
when willing members are energetically involved,
and
when the Bible passage and method are well chosen:
THEN you are ready for a good group experience!

Worksheet for small group leaders
Preparing for the meeting

1. *People:*

Who is coming and why? List all the people coming, with one need or prayer request for each person. Pray for each person, and for the group as a whole.

2. *Arrangements:*

What needs to be done to prepare for the time together? What arrangements need to be made about the meeting place, seating, Bibles, temperature, food, looking after the children, music, materials, etc.? Who will do it? Are you sure?

3. *Relationships:*

How will you help people to feel cared for and caring? What will you do to help build positive relationships among the members of the group? (Sharing question, relational exercise, checking-in, names, etc.)

4. *Study/Task:*

What steps will you follow to accomplish the task or complete the study? List the questions you will use, and estimate the amount of time for discussing each one.

5. *Prayer:*

What are your goals for the prayer time? How much time? What kind of prayer? Who will pray, when? How will you accomplish these goals?

6. *Time:*

What time is available and how will you divide it up? Block out the time available into major segments and indicate the activity to be done in each segment. What is your "real" starting time? Your firm closing time? How will you open and close each segment? Are you attempting too much? Too little? Do you want to ask people to take responsibility for various segments?

4

Preparing for Bible Study

What part of the Bible shall we study and how shall we study it?

The Bible is a collection of writings of many different types. There is historical narrative and biography as well as poetry and wisdom literature. There are letters and Gospels, prophecies and psalms.

Choosing a section of Scripture to focus upon is the first step in using the Bible in groups. The purpose of the group will help determine this decision.

Because the Bible is a collection of books, the most basic pattern of Bible study is to study one book at a time. Within a book the most convenient unit of study is the chapter. Studying one or two verses is seldom adequate to grasp the thought of the writer and interpret it properly in context. Larger units of study such as the paragraph and the chapter give more with which to interact. Even if thematic or topical study is the method used, the basic building block of study should be more than a single verse or two. The Bible was written in large sections. It is best read and studied that way.

CHOOSING WHAT TO STUDY

The following biblical material has been found to be useful in small groups:

O **Books of the Bible** or selected sections of longer books of the Bible. Especially useful in groups are the Gospels, Acts, the letters of Paul, Peter, James and John; Genesis 1 – 12 and 12 – 50; Exodus 1 – 20; Ruth; Nehemiah; Psalms; the Minor Prophets, especially Amos, Hosea, Micah, Jonah, and Habakkuk; and portions of the Major Prophets. Old Testament material usually means providing group members with somewhat more historical background than may be required for most New Testament studies.

O **Biographies of Bible characters:** e.g. Abraham, Moses, Deborah, David, Ruth, Peter and Paul.

O **Great chapters of the Bible:** Genesis 1; Exodus 19 – 20; Exodus 32; Isaiah 53; Acts 2; 1 Corinthians 13 and 15; Romans 8; Galatians 5; Ephesians 2; Philippians 2; Revelation 21.

O   Encounters with Jesus in the Gospel of John: the first disciples (John 1.35-51); Nicodemus (3.1-21); the Samaritan woman (4.1-42); the healing at the pool of Bethseda (5.1-18); the woman caught in adultery (8.1-11); the man born blind (9.1-34); the death of Lazarus (11.1-44); Mary Magdalene (20.1-18); Peter (21.1-19).

O   Great sections of the Bible: the Sermon on the Mount (Matthew 5 – 7); discourses in the Upper Room (John 13 – 17); Isaiah 40 – 55; Letters to the Churches (Revelation 1 – 3).

O   Great prayers of the Bible: Genesis 18, 32; Exodus 32; 1 Samuel 2; Psalm 51, 139; 1 Kings 3, 19; 2 Kings 6.8-23, 18-19; 2 Chronicles 6, 20; Nehemiah 9; Isaiah 6.1-8; Jeremiah 1.1-10; Jonah 2; Ephesians 1.15-23, 3.14-19; Philippians 1.3-5, 9-11; Colossians 1.3-5, 9-14; 1 Thessalonians 1.2-3, 5.23-25; 2 Thessalonians 1.11-12, 3.1-2; Philemon 4-6; Hebrews 13.20-21.

O   Major themes of the Bible: poverty and riches; suffering and evil; bondage and freedom; law and grace; covenants old and new; creation old and new; the kingdom of God; the day of the Lord; discipleship – call, faith and obedience; the gospel to all the nations; the second coming of Christ; holiness; salvation; the Suffering Servant; images of the Church – the body of Christ, the household of faith, the temple of God, etc.

O   Specific topics in the Bible: families in the Bible; women in the Bible; marriage in the Bible; leadership in the Old and New Testaments; Satan and the demonic; healing; spiritual gifts; knowing the will of God; temptation and trial; ministry; fasting; confessions; conflicts in the Bible, etc.

O   Psalms and Proverbs: Psalms 1, 8, 19, 23, 25, 32, 34, 37, 42, 51, 62, 73, 107, 121; Proverbs 1 – 7, 10 – 19, 31; and many other psalms and proverbs are also useful for group study.

O   Word studies: faith; salvation; justification; grace; mercy; redemption; perseverance; love; hope; peace; Holy Spirit; obedience; gifts; baptism; patience; renewal; forgiveness; sanctification.

Planning a series

A common pattern for discipleship groups or new groups to use is as follows:

1. A study of a Gospel. Usually the Gospel of Mark is chosen because of its brevity and directness in telling the story of Jesus. This is a good place to begin, because of the centrality of Jesus in Christian faith. Mark is a simpler book to study than the Gospel of John with its more complex theological reflection. A group planning to meet for eight weeks may want to study one chapter a week, or some part of each chapter for eight weeks, so that the first half of the Gospel is completed by the end of the group time. If the group chooses to continue meeting for another eight weeks, the second half of the book can be completed.

2. A study of the early Christians. Acts introduces issues related to the Holy Spirit, the beginnings of the Church, life together, the expansion of Christianity and the story of key early Christian leaders including Paul, Stephen, Philip and Barnabas. Most groups will prefer to study key sections of Acts in detail with an emphasis on the first ten chapters, and simply get an overview study of the rest of the book.

3. A study of one of the letters to young churches. For example, Philippians, Ephesians, Galatians, or 1 Peter. These letters raise crucial questions of faith and life as experienced in the early churches and relevant to life today. Because of the density of the material in these letters, usually two weeks per chapter is needed.

After these foundation studies, groups can go in a variety of directions. Many will choose to do an Old Testament study next, either choosing a book study such as Genesis or the first twenty chapters of Exodus, or a biographical study of an Old Testament character such as Abraham, David, or Ruth. Others may prefer to work in the Psalms or Proverbs. An alternating pattern of study in the Old Testament and then New Testament can become a profitable rhythm of study for groups over many years.

The choice of what to study should be made with the backgrounds and interests of the group members in mind. It may not be productive to spend a great deal of time on material that members find "overfamiliar". To choose material that is too difficult or lengthy may discourage some. The amount of Bible background, personal Bible study and desire to learn that the group members have should be taken into account. Do not begin with books that are too difficult and complex such as Revelation or Ezekiel. Groups can easily get bogged down trying to work with this type of material. Even people who have been long-time church members often do not have a clear idea of what the Gospels say or what the letters of Paul or Peter mean. Do not assume more knowledge than most of the group members are likely to have.

Tools for choosing and understanding Bible passages

Here are some basic tools for Bible study which are helpful in choosing topics and in understanding the text:

O   One or more contemporary **translations** of the Bible. One advantage of having more than one version is that you can compare translations to help you understand the text.

O   A **study Bible** includes aids to understanding such as maps, word lists, chronologies, cross-references, and subject indexes. The *Good News Bible* contains examples of these.

O   An English language **dictionary** is needed to give help in looking up words where the meaning is unclear.

O   A **concordance** to the Bible. This is a tool which lists alphabetically every word which appears in the Bible and all the passages using that word. A shortened or concise concordance lists all the major words with the key references where they occur. This is very helpful in designing topical, thematic or word studies. For instance, if you want to study "faith", you can look that word up in the concordance, and find where the word is used in Scripture. Decide which verses are significant for group study and arrange them in an appropriate order. Most concordances include lists of names with references to where those names are found. This is helpful in designing a biographical study. There are concordances for use with the *Authorized Version*, the *Revised Standard Version*, the *New International Version* and the *Good News Bible*. The *Concordance to the Good News Bible* contains a Thematic Index, which directs the reader to related words. This is especially useful for thematic studies.

The following are also helpful:

O   A **handbook** to the Bible. This gives you brief introductions to each book of the Bible and often contains useful information about historical circumstances, archeological findings, and customs of Bible peoples.

O   A **Bible dictionary**. This tool gives you in alphabetical order an introduction to every major word, person, or event in the Bible. This is a very helpful way to gather basic information with some, although minimal, interpretative content.

Commentaries

In most small groups it is not helpful to use commentaries on the Bible, because group members can rely overmuch on the commentator instead of working with the text themselves. Reading from commentaries in a small group is likely to destroy lively discussion. In addition, all commentaries are written from a perspective which shapes the interpretation given to the text. If a group leader or member wishes to consult commentaries, they should do so only after the completion of a careful and thorough personal study. It is important to remember that while commentaries are systematic reflections on the Scriptures, they do not have the same inspiration and authority that Scripture itself has.

CHOOSING THE BIBLE STUDY METHOD

After choosing the passages of Scripture and the tools you will use, you are almost ready to choose the particular method(s) of Bible study.

First, however, it is helpful to understand the basic stages or processes common to all methods of interaction with Scripture. Just as a cook uses and varies basic processes like baking, boiling, or frying in many different recipes, so the Bible study leader will use the same basic processes in varying ways in order to study the Bible.

Three common stages in all Bible methods

All methods of interaction with the Scripture contain these three basic stages or processes:

1. The passage(s) of Scripture chosen must be introduced.
2. There must be group interaction with the passage.
3. An opportunity should be given for some personal reaction or response to the passage.

Each of these stages can be handled in a variety of ways, as shown below.

Stage 1: Introducing the text

How will the passage of Scripture be introduced? Possibilities include:
O   silent reading of the text by all
O   oral reading of the text by one member, or in turns
O   group oral reading of the text in unison or antiphonally (alternating verses and readers)
O   a role-playing or dramatization of the text
O   copying the text
O   hearing or singing a song, hymn or oratorio which uses the text
O   reciting a text which has been previously memorized
O   viewing works of art based upon the text.

Stage 2: Interacting with the text

How will the group interact with the passage? Possibilities for this include:
O   asking and answering questions about it individually and together
O   sharing answers to questions worked on before the group meeting

O   individual and/or group paraphrasing or restatement of the text in their own words
O   discussing issues arising from the text
O   group or sub-group dramatization of the passage
O   creative movement expressing the feelings conveyed or stirred up by the passage, e.g. in the Psalms
O   doing individual and group study of the passage such as listing characters, defining terms, identifying elements in the text like comparisons, contrasts, repetitions, instructions; using resources to aid in the interaction with the text such as concordances, Bible atlases, Bible dictionaries, and commentaries
O   meditation upon the passage and a sharing of the results with other group members
O   when the text is a story, retelling the story in fresh words
O   listing the issues raised by the text and discussing contemporary attitudes and responses to these issues, etc.

Stage 3: Responding to the text

How will members be helped to respond to the passage? Possibilities here include:
O   application questions (see page 59) to be discussed together or thought about individually
O   adopting spiritual disciplines which aid the application of biblical truth, such as prayer, keeping a journal, financial giving, time spent in service, personal Bible study, etc.
O   Scripture response exercises; mission or action discussions and assignments
O   accountability questions (see page 104)
O   mission questions
O   relational exercises
O   times of silence
O   individual and corporate prayer, etc.

Once it is understood that all groups which use the Bible have only three basic questions to answer about each passage, choosing the particular methods to be used is simplified. To summarize, these three questions are: How shall we introduce the passage? How shall we interact with the passage? How shall we respond to the passage?

New ways of studying the passage may be discovered simply by mixing and matching the items in the first stage with items in the second and third stages. No one arrangement of stages is necessarily superior to the others.

The methods that you choose should be shaped by the purpose of the group, its level of experience in Bible study, and the amount of time available for interacting with the Scriptures.

CONDUCTING THE STUDY

Whatever method of Bible study you choose for use in the group, certain basic principles are common to all:

1. Good group Bible studies are discussions not lectures. The joy of discovery in Bible study comes as each member searches the Scriptures personally and has an opportunity to discuss and interact with other group members. This moves

members from being passive to being active and the Bible study becomes a life-changing experience. Good Bible study leaders therefore should not dominate the discussion by displaying their own knowledge and insight. They should seek to help group members discover for themselves what the Bible says and how it can be applied to life.

2. **The secret of good Bible study is knowing how to ask the right kinds of questions.** Questions fall into three main categories. They ask for information (i.e. observations), interpretation, or application:

O   What does the passage say? What information is given and what are the facts in this passage?

O   What is the meaning of this passage? What was the original author's purpose in writing this?

O   How and in what way is the passage relevant today? Of what value is it? How do we apply the passage to life today?

These questions of observation, interpretation, and application are essential to all thoughtful interaction with the Scripture.

3. **The ultimate aim of group Bible study is application, not just the accumulation of knowledge.** The goal is not to settle every question or deal with every possible issue which the Scripture might raise, but to respond in obedience to the central truth or truths in the passage. The danger is that groups may go off at tangents trying to solve all the problems in the text, and miss hearing and responding to the truth which is clearly stated.

There are also some helpful ground rules:

1. **Each person should have his or her own copy of the text.**

2. **Usually each study should begin with a reading of the selected portion of Scripture.** Do not assume that people have read the passage at home and therefore do not need to read or hear it read again. Reading the Scripture together, whether silently or aloud, helps focus the group before they begin discussion. A brief time of silence while members read and reflect helps each one to "centre in", thus moving away from pressures and distractions.

3. **Use silence creatively.** Bible studies often feel too rushed when there is no time taken to think about what is being read or discussed. Consider including a time of silence when people may reflect, write, meditate, or pray about their response to Scripture. There is a difference between a productive "filled" silence and the awkward silence that comes when no one knows what to say or do. Help people use silence productively by providing a focus for reflection or a suggestion about how to use the time.

4. **Involve as many of the senses as possible:** i.e. sight, through each one reading the text; sound, as the text is read aloud; touch, through writing, either copying a part or a whole of the text or writing a response to the passage. Try to involve the whole person, through discussion or through the use of imagination or dramatization in reconstructing a story or scene from Scripture; consider the value of memorizing and reciting a verse or singing a psalm or hymn which restates biblical truth. The greater the involvement, the deeper the impression made.

5. **Stay in one passage.** When discussing a passage, do not jump around in the Bible from one section to another, either by casually quoting other passages or by quickly moving from one verse to another, when they are in different parts of the Bible. Try to stay focused on one section of Scripture at a time. Otherwise you will discourage beginners as well as tend to encourage a superficial treatment of

the passage before you. If moving from one passage to another is necessary to the topic under discussion, make sure that all members of the group look at each of the passages being discussed.

6. **Avoid boring Bible study through variety.** Doing exactly the same thing in precisely the same way every week can become tedious. Even if you are using the same basic pattern of study each week, consider occasional changes. For example, begin rather than end the meeting with a time of prayer, introduce the study differently, or try a new method of approach from time to time. One advantage of passing the leadership around is that a different person asks the questions each week. Good application questions also promote interesting discussions which shift from theoretical to practical concerns.

GROUP PURPOSES AND METHODS OF STUDY

Four primary purposes for Bible study seem to emerge as groups make decisions about what methods to adopt. The way that groups mix and match the stages of Bible study will relate directly to this. While each group may be interested in all the purposes, usually one is more important or more central to how the group wants to use its time. The four purposes relate specifically to what the group wants to happen in and through its interaction with the Scripture. The purposes are:

O   To study Scripture in a systematic way through observation, interpretation and application.

O   To read and respond to Scripture without much emphasis on methodical approaches to study of the text.

O   To encounter the text in deep, personally involving ways so as to enter into its meaning and application at more than a superficial or intellectual level.

O   To search the Scripture for direction and encouragement in Christian mission or action.

Each one of these primary purposes has a set of methods particularly appropriate to accomplish that purpose. When you have decided on the primary purpose for your group's use of the Bible, review the methods most suited to that purpose, and choose one or more for use.

The four sets of methods

1. Those which seek to study Scripture to gain knowledge, understanding and direction for living. These are the basic methods chosen by most new groups in the beginning. These methods require thirty to sixty minutes to be available for group focus on the Scripture.

2. Those which focus on responding to Scripture through personal reflection or group discussion. These methods assume a general familiarity with the Scripture. It is assumed that people already know the basic facts of the passage and the meaning intended by the author, so that the group time can be spent on the personal response and application stage. Group time focused directly on Scripture ranges from fifteen to thirty minutes.

3. Those which seek an in-depth encounter with Scripture through imagination, psychological insight, drama or meditation. These groups usually require a fairly sophisticated or intensely committed group, with a well-prepared leader or well-developed written guides as a resource. These can be intensely moving, deeply compelling encounters with Scripture. Time required would seldom be

less than an hour – perhaps more.

4. Those which focus on action by searching Scripture to direct and encourage ministry. These methods presuppose a general knowledge and overview of Scripture which allows for a choosing of particular passages without taking them seriously out of context and distorting their teaching. Group time spent on interaction with Scripture would range from fifteen to forty-five minutes.

The key words to summarize the focus of each set of methods are:
O   Study
O   Response
O   Encounter
O   Action.

It is important to notice that most small groups will include elements from more than one set of methods. The descriptions are useful as a way of thinking about the overall direction which the group wishes to take.

OVERVIEW OF BIBLE STUDY METHODS

Set One   Methods of interacting with Scripture which focus on study. There is one basic method used in this group – the inductive or "discovery" method of Bible study. This method is applied to different materials with some variations but following a similar pattern in each case.
1. Discovery study
2. Chapter study
3. Book study
4. Thematic or topical study
5. Word study
6. Biographical study

Advantages
O   Careful attention to the text overcomes superficial or misleading first impressions, counters biblical illiteracy, and provides a common base of knowledge and understanding before moving to necessarily diverse applications.
O   Encourages personal Bible study by providing a system and method of digging into the text which people can use without prior training.
O   Takes Scripture seriously by examining it on its own terms without imposing categories or personal impressions before making sure that the text has been carefully reviewed.
O   Can build genuine excitement as people discover for themselves the meaning and relevance of the Bible.

Disadvantages
O   Can become impersonal, dry, and uninteresting if the discussion moves too slowly or bogs down in detail rather than briskly moving through the material.
O   If time is not managed well, all the time can be taken for questions of observation and interpretation and no time will be left for application.
O   Danger of purely idea-oriented study.
O   Can provide opportunity for those with more background to show off their knowledge or dominate those less informed.

Suitable for almost all types of biblical material.

Set Two Methods of interacting with Scripture which centre in response.

7. Devotional study: reading, reflection and reaction
8. Paraphrasing and response
9. Exploring personal problems in the light of Scripture
10. Relational Bible study (dealing with the discovery and building of relationships)

Advantages

O   Allows for a focus on Scripture even when time is very limited.

O   Encourages personal involvement with the text as participants consider the text in relation to their own lives.

O   Reminds people of truths they have known, and these truths are reinforced in their lives.

O   A relatively low-key approach that requires less preparation than "study" methods. If people are already quite well informed about the background to the passage, these are the easiest and least complex methods.

Disadvantages

O   If the passage is not previously known or easily understood, these methods can become a sharing of ignorance, inviting a subjective response to things which may not even be present in the text.

O   Limited time sometimes encourages a shallow or superficial reading of Scripture.

O   A focus on response may reinforce pre-existent opinions but may not challenge or change them to any great degree.

O   The time available may limit the type of passage that can be examined.

Many kinds of biblical literature cannot be examined profitably through these methods.

Set Three Methods of interacting with Scripture which focus on depth encounter and total involvement with the text.

11. Feelings and faith: encounter with the Psalms
12. Depth and encounter
13. Transformational Bible study
14. You are there: role-playing and dramatization
15. Knowing God and ourselves: meditation
16. Sing a joyful song: singing or listening, writing or playing

Advantages

O   These methods encourage people to express themselves in more ways than just talking.

O   Deliberate efforts to engage the person's feelings may overcome long-standing barriers and resistances to faith.

O   People who are more oriented to physical or psychological expression may find these methods helpful when more traditional methods appear boring or uninvolving.

O   High excitement and energy may be released.

O   Lasting and deep impressions are often made.

Disadvantages

O   Inexperience with the methods may lead to awkwardness and uneasiness or anxiety unless methods are expertly led.

O   People not comfortable with making immediate applications may resist sharing without more time for reflection.

O   Some may feel timid if the contribution of others is weak or songs are not well known.

Types of Scripture especially suitable for these methods include the narratives and parables of Jesus, and prophetic materials and stories in the Old Testament. Less suitable are extended instructional sections, such as Romans, or historical summaries.

Set Four   Methods of interacting with Scripture which focus on action.

17. Preparing for action: concerning hunger, poverty, evangelism, justice, community, peace-making, obedience, suffering, church growth, etc.

18.Current events and Christian action

19. Practising accountability: "Doing the Word" (acting upon learning)

20. Disciplines and decision: choosing and using spiritual disciplines

Advantages

O   Time spent in reflecting upon the Scriptures can help deepen, encourage, and maintain the energy and commitment needed for action – otherwise action groups without a strong spiritual focus may find themselves becoming dry, bitter, cynical, or depressed under the stress of service.

O   Wisdom and guidance for the work can come from Scripture.

O   A vital personal relationship to God can be nourished. As Jesus said: "You can do nothing without me" (John 15.5). Time spent in Scripture can enable the work to be done effectively.

Disadvantages

O   Too much study can become an excuse for too little action, just as a commitment to action can crowd out meaningful times of study, prayer and sharing. Action groups must therefore strike a balance between study, prayer, sharing and action.

O   A limited amount of time spent in Scripture at each meeting may become perfunctory and meaningless unless careful attention is paid to keeping this part of the group fresh.

O   The same question asked each week can lead to staleness and a flattening of response and growth.

The focus of the Scripture passages will usually be on the Gospels, the Prophets, or on exhortative sections of the Letters, as well as thematic or topical studies drawing from many parts of Scripture. Some action groups find the Psalms a helpful resource.

Some criteria for choosing a method or materials

O   How much true study of the Bible will actually occur as a result of this method or these materials? Who will study, who will learn, how much, and with what results?

O   How will this method of group study help to build good Bible study habits and patterns into people's daily lives? Can this method be used individually?

O   Which method of Bible study will help the group of people you are working with to have the best foundation for faith and become more mature Christians in the long run? Does the method encourage dependence on leaders or printed resources? What expense is involved?

SUMMARY
While there are many other methods of using the Bible, chapters 5 and 6 present the twenty methods outlined in this chapter. They should offer a good beginning and possibilities for future involvement for many years.

5

Bible Study Methods in Small Groups

Study Methods
1. Discovery Bible study
2. Chapter study
3. Book study
4. Thematic or topical study
5. Word study
6. Biographical study

Set One: Methods focused on Study
The following methods are the most demanding methods in terms of preparation and effort. Many people find that these methods are the most rewarding because so much is learned.

1. DISCOVERY BIBLE STUDY
This is the basic method of inductive Bible study, which provides a foundation for almost all other methods of interaction with Scripture. The basic steps are:

Preparation
The leader chooses a compact section of Scripture, usually one or two paragraphs in length, and studies the passage carefully using the tools of:
O   Observation – looking at the facts contained in the passage and what is happening.
O   Interpretation – determining the author's meaning and purpose.
O   Application – the relevance of this passage for contemporary faith and life.
   The leader then either uses a study guide which lists questions for discussion, or develops his or her own set of questions for the group discussion. A thirty-minute discussion time might use between five and seven questions. Forty-five to sixty minutes might use from seven to ten questions.

Procedure

1. Group members are asked either to read the assigned passage in silence, or to listen and follow the text as one group member reads it aloud. Members are asked to think about a question as they read or as they listen.

Examples Let us read silently Ephesians 2.1-10. As you read, look for any comparisons or contrasts in this section.

Or: Let us listen as Tom reads Mark 2.1-12. As we listen, try to identify the various people who are present and what feelings they are likely to have.

2. The group leader asks questions for discussion. The questions are of three basic types:

Observation questions

Observation questions seek to **discover the facts and structure** of the passage.

Examples Mark 2.1-12: Who are the people in this story, and what do we learn from the text about each of them?

Ephesians 2.1-10: What is the contrast in these verses, and what are the differences between the two things contrasted?

Psalm 37: What exhortations does the psalmist give, and what are the reasons he gives for keeping each one?

Questions to ask when seeking to stimulate observation in a passage:
O   What are the basic facts in this passage?
O   Who, what, where, why and when?
O   What do you notice about the way in which this passage is written?
O   What repetitions, comparisons and contrasts, verb tenses, use of conjunctions, cause and effect, logical constructions are present?
O   What kind of literature is this (e.g. history, teaching material, poetry, prophecy, story, etc.)?

Like a detective on the scene of a crime, a significant amount of time is spent gathering the facts before attempting to draw conclusions. This can become very exciting as people learn really to "see" the text as they never have seen the Bible before.

Observations should **launch** students into a careful examination of the text to see exactly what material it contains as a foundation for interpretation.

Interpretation questions

These are questions to help the group discover the meaning of the text and to understand the purpose of the original author.

Examples Mark 2.1-12: Why does Jesus speak to the paralysed man about sin before dealing with his physical need? Why does he heal the paralysed man?

Ephesians 2.1-10: What does it mean to be spiritually "dead" and "alive"? What are the sources of influence on each? How do you define in your own words "grace" and "faith"?

Psalm 37: Who are the "good" and who are the "wicked"? What does the psalmist believe about each? Why does the psalmist believe that his readers should trust in the Lord?

Interpretation questions should help members **explore** the meaning of the passage. Common interpretative questions are:

○ Why?
○ Are there any words or phrases which need definition?
○ How do we define these terms?
○ What is the significance of any of the observations we have made?
○ Is there any progression or logical development of significance in this passage?
○ What is the main point of this passage?
○ What was the author trying to get across in this passage?
○ What is the most important thing this passage communicates?
○ How would you summarize what this passage teaches?

Application questions

Application questions seek to help group members **integrate** the personal meaning and relevance of the text into their own lives. These questions seek to bridge the gap between "then and there" to talk about "here and now".

Examples Mark 2.1-12: Jesus talks about his ability to forgive sins. Do you think forgiveness of sins is a need that people have today? Why, or why not? Is this a need you have experienced in your own life? How, if ever, has forgiveness been important to you?

Ephesians 2.1-10: Has there ever been a "before" and "after" in your own spiritual life? What made the difference for you? What are some of the "good works" which you believe Christians should be engaged in as a result of God's grace?

Psalm 37: Where do you find yourself tending to worry and how does the psalmist "speak to your condition"? Where do you find his counsel easy and where do you find it difficult?

Application questions ask:
○ What issues does this passage raise which are still issues today?
○ What does the passage say about God, about people, about sin, about salvation, about living?
○ How do we appropriate and apply this today?
○ How do we build into our lives the truths in this text? When? Where?
○ How does this passage challenge our contemporary values and life-style?
○ What behaviour does this passage call for?
○ How do we put into practice what we are learning?

Most inductive studies include three or four observation questions, intermixed with three or four interpretation questions, and followed by one or two application questions which may be asked in discussion or given for silent and/or written reflection.

Keys to success

○ Ask observation and interpretation questions which are clearly tied to the text and which build logically upon one another.
○ Limit questions to key information and definitions. You can't discuss everything. Focus upon the most important.
○ If someone doesn't understand your question, be prepared to re-state it once in different words. If no one gets it then, give it up and go on to the next question. Never answer questions yourself.
○ After the first response, ask if anyone noticed anything else or has

anything to add. Wait. After brief discussion, go on to the next question. Don't wait until everything possible has been said before moving on.

O   It helps to mention the verses where the answers can be found: e.g. In verses 2 and 3 of Ephesians 2, what does Paul say is the problem with those who are "spiritually dead"? In verse 8 what do you think Paul means by "saved through faith"?

O   Move through the questions at a relatively brisk pace, making sure that adequate time is reserved for application.

Resources

This method is easiest for beginners to use when an inductive discussion study guide is available for the particular part of Scripture which you are studying. Neighborhood Bible Studies in Dobbs Ferry, New York, has helpful discussion guides available for almost all books of the Bible. Other resources are mentioned in the Bibliography. You can write your own questions, but it does take time and some experience.

If a study guide is available, the leader should work through its questions to decide which ones should be used in a particular meeting. Most guides have many more questions than can be used in the time available.

See the examples of discovery studies.

Example 1

Discovery Study: 2 Corinthians 1.3-11

Personal preparation: (3-5 minutes)

Read silently through this passage from the apostle Paul to the Christians at Corinth. As you read, look for repetitions, comparisons and contrasts.

Group discussion: (30-40 minutes)

1 a) What are the most frequent repetitions in verses 3-7? What comparisons or contrasts do you notice?

b) What repetitions, comparisons or contrasts do you observe in verses 8-11?

2 a) What does it mean to say that "He [God] helps us in all our troubles"? Why do people need comforting?

b) What kind of troubles has Paul experienced and how has this affected him?

c) What kind of troubles and sufferings do Christians experience in which they need the comfort of God?

3. What are to be the results of having received comfort? What do verses 3-11 tell us the characteristics of the Christian community are to be?

4. Notice Paul's mention of "hope" in verses 7 and 10? What are the reasons for Paul's hope? What has Paul learned about God?

5. When, if ever, have you needed and received the comfort of God? When, if ever, have you shared the comfort of God with another person?

6. Why does Paul ask the Corinthians to pray for him (verse 11)? Why is prayer important in the Christian community?

7. What encouragement and hope can you draw from this passage for our Christian living today?

8. (optional) Is there any area in which you are living under pressure or troubles or are suffering, about which you would like to ask for prayer so that we may pray for each other?

Example 2
Inductive (Discovery) Study: Mark 2.1-12

First, make sure everyone has a Bible open at Mark. Then, ask someone to read aloud Mark 2.1-12. Next, move through the paragraph by discussing the following questions:

1. Where and why does the crowd gather?

2. What indications of Jesus' popularity are there at this time.

3. Why and how is Jesus' preaching interrupted? What is his reaction to this interruption?

4. What do you think the paralysed man's friends have in mind? Compare with what Jesus says in verse 5.

5. Who reacts to this statement? How? Why? Look up "scribes" and "blasphemy" in a dictionary. Under Jewish law, blasphemy was punishable by death.

6. In your own words what are the scribes saying? How does Jesus answer? What is the point of Jesus' question in verse 9?

7. What does Jesus expect to prove to the scribes by healing the paralysed man?

8. How does the paralysed man express his faith? What are the reactions to his healing? With whom do the people connect the healing?

9. All those present heard Jesus' words of forgiveness but how many were actually forgiven? What implications does that have for us today?

Conclude the study of Mark 2.1-12 by suggesting some applications:

The paralysed man needed his four friends to help bring him to Jesus. However, the man himself eventually had to respond in faith to Jesus' command. His friends could not help him then. Others may help us to learn about Jesus, but the time soon comes when each must respond to him either in faith or in unbelief.

In this incident Jesus stated his authority (the right and the power) to forgive sins. Have you considered that he can do this for you?

Sometimes we may have the opportunity to play the part of these friends. As in this case, it will cost time and energy and perhaps more. Who, do you think, paid for the roof?

End with a brief prayer by the leader or sentence prayers by group members.

(Source: Marilyn Kunz and Kay Schell, *How to Start a Neighborhood Bible Study,* Neighborhood Bible Studies, Box 222, Dobbs Ferry, NY 10522, 1966)

Example 3
Discovery Study: Ephesians 2.1-10

Read through the first ten verses of chapter two of Ephesians noticing the contrast between "dead" and "alive".

1. What is the contrast in these verses between "dead" and "alive"? Who was dead? Who is alive? What was true of them when they were dead? What facts are stated about them now that they are alive? (Simply mention the relevant words and phrases – do not discuss in detail.)

2. What does it mean to be "spiritually dead because of your disobedience and sins"? What are the sources of influence on the "dead" person mentioned in verses 2 and 3? (Or: What three things does the "dead" person follow?) What are the results of following these influences? In everyday language according to this passage: What is deadness? What are its causes and who does it involve?

3. From verses 4-7: How has God made a difference for dead people? What has God done for us? Why? At what stage in our existence does God love us? . . . after we have sorted ourselves out? What does it mean to say that God loved us even when we were dead? What implications does this have for God's attitude towards those who are not now Christians?

4. According to verses 8 and 9, what is the relationship between God's work and our efforts to accomplish our salvation? What are some of the "works" that people do to win salvation or the approval of God? What is "grace"? What is "faith"? What does it mean in your own words to say "For it is by God's grace that you have been saved through faith"? How do we obtain salvation? How do we get from being dead to being alive? What is our part? What is God's part?

5. According to verse 10, what is the purpose for which God has made us alive? What does it mean to say "God has made us what we are"? What do you think are the good deeds which God expects of those whom he has made alive?

6. From the passage as a whole, what do you learn about God? What do you learn about the situation of mankind without God? How do you respond to this passage?

7. How would you describe your present situation in life? Dead? Alive? Somewhere in the middle? How can you experience being alive in God? If you are alive in God, what is expected of you in response to his action for you? What specific good works do you think you should be doing this week. When will you begin? What help do you need?

2. CHAPTER STUDY

Preparation
The leader chooses the chapter for study and prepares a worksheet for group members to use. The worksheet is on one page, and each group member needs a copy (see page 65). Group members may complete the worksheets as homework and bring them to the group meeting, or they may take fifteen to twenty minutes at the beginning of the group time for silent study, filling out the worksheet.

Procedure
The group may be split into fours or stay together as a large group to discuss the chapter and what each has written on their worksheets. Each person should be given an opportunity to share their findings on at least one question. Questions for discussion (to be asked and discussed one question at a time):
O   What title did you give to the chapter and to the paragraphs?
O   What key words and phrases did you identify and what is their meaning and significance?
O   What is the main point or central lesson of this chapter as you see it?
O   What difficulties or questions did the chapter raise for you? Take group time to discuss these. Did anyone else have the same difficulty or question? How do you respond to it?
O   Is there anything in this chapter that is important for faith and life today? Where and how should the insights and teachings of this chapter be applied in our lives?

Keys to success
O   Each person must have a worksheet and something to write with, a comfortable place to work and a copy of the chapter.
O   Instructions should be clear and the amount of time available for study announced.
O   Notice should be given about two minutes before ending the study time to allow people a chance to work on other parts of the worksheet.
O   During the discussion, breaking into smaller groups allows for more discussion and sharing of findings than can be accomplished if the whole group stays together. The leader may wish to break into smaller groups for the first four discussion questions and then bring the whole group together for the last two questions.

Resources
See the example of a chapter chart.

Chapter chart for _____

Chapter _____

Chapter title _____

_____

Paragraph titles (3-4 words)

vv. _____

vv. _____

vv. _____

vv. _____

vv. _____

Key verse _____

Summary or outline

Key words and phrases
· Main point or central lesson

Key words and phrases

Difficulties or questions

Application

3. BOOK STUDY

Preparation

Choose a book brief enough for the group to complete its study in the number of weeks that are available. The leader should read the book at least three times well ahead of the first group meeting.

After reading the book, divide it up into "chewable bites" or manageable segments for each week's meeting. Usually this will involve one or two weeks per chapter, depending on the density and complexity of the biblical material. An example of how to divide up or "block out" a book can be seen on the worksheet for 1 Thessalonians. One good pattern in book studies looks like this:

Week one: Get an overview of the book by skim reading it, taking a careful look at the introduction and concluding sections of the book. People are encouraged to see the book as a whole – identifying the author, audience, setting, obvious main themes, purpose of the book (if easily discernable), main sections of the book, discussing first impressions.

Week two to eight or nine: Study the book section by section from the first to the final chapter, using discovery or chapter study methods.

Final week: Review the book by examining any themes that run through the whole book, summarizing its main teachings, and discussing application of the central ideas to personal and group faith and life.

Each week, the leader prepares a set of discussion questions appropriate to the study task of the evening.

Procedure

1. The first session might be introduced in this way:

Tonight we are going to begin our study of Paul's Letter to the Galatians. Let's pretend that this piece of ancient parchment has just been found in the back of a cave in the area near the Dead Sea. Word has leaked to the world press, who are waiting anxiously for a press conference in which we will tell them what has been discovered in this ancient document. They are eager to hear from us, so let's take ten or fifteen minutes to read rapidly through this whole letter to discover everything we can about it in the time available. Reading it as if we had never seen it before, try to find out what you can about the author, the recipients, why the letter was written and what it is about.

2. After ten or so minutes, the leader asks: What have you learned?

3. After a discussion of first impressions, which might take ten to twenty minutes, the leader says: Now let us look at the first paragraph of the letter, to learn what we can from it. What are the facts given there? Then . . . let us look at the concluding section of the letter. What do we learn from this? Then . . . in future weeks we will be looking in more detail at each of the sections of this letter. Next week we will be studying chapter 1 verses 6-24.

Keys to success

O In studying a book, beware of getting bogged down in too many details, or the study can become boring.

O Moving as rapidly as possible while doing justice to the material requires careful planning of how much material will be covered in each session. Book studies that never end or that stop without finishing the book discourage members.

O   The leader may need to summarize some sections of the book in a brief statement and then focus the group discussion on a key paragraph or story for the discussion time. Even if some material in the middle of the book has to be handled superficially, plan to finish the book with at least one discussion on the last chapter and summary of major themes. This gives a sense of success and finality to the group's work.

Resource
See the example of the book study on 1 Thessalonians.

Example

Book Study: 1 Thessalonians

The purpose of the Bible study portion of the small group meeting is to concentrate on a brief portion of Scripture as an aid to Christian growth and prayer. This is not a detailed study but a focus of thought to shape our prayer and life together.

The first letter to the Thessalonians was written only twenty years after the crucifixion of Jesus. The apostle Paul wrote to this church in northern Greece which he had founded with his associates Silas and Timothy.

Suggested passages for study:

Week 1:	Introduction and overview	Why this letter?
Week 2:	1 Thessalonians 1	Faith, hope and love
Week 3:	1 Thessalonians 2.1-9	Sharing the gospel and life
Week 4:	1 Thessalonians 2.10-20	Receiving the Word of God
Week 5:	1 Thessalonians 3	Standing firm in the Lord
Week 6:	1 Thessalonians 4.1-12	Living to please God
Week 7:	1 Thessalonians 4.13-18	The coming of the Lord
Week 8:	1 Thessalonians 5.1-11	Belonging to the day
Week 9:	1 Thessalonians 5.12-28	God's will for you
Week 10:	Review (skim read whole book)	Encouraging one another

Suggested pattern of study:

1. To begin the Bible study period, the leader asks the group members to read the assigned passage through silently, looking for the key verse or idea. More than one key idea may emerge. Allow several minutes of silence.

2. Ask one person to read the passage aloud from a contemporary version.

3. Ask: a) What is the key verse or idea in this passage and why do you think it is? (i.e. What evidence supports your conclusion?)

b) What do you learn about Paul and about the Thessalonian Christians?

c) What do you learn about God/Christ/the Holy Spirit in this passage?

d) What do you learn about living the Christian life?

e) How does this passage question you? What challenges you, threatens you, inspires you, examines you?

f) What ideas for prayer does this passage suggest?

If there is a very limited time for study, do the silent reading and only questions a) and e). Remember the purpose: to listen to Scripture to aid our life and prayer.

4. THEMATIC OR TOPICAL STUDY

Preparation

After the theme or topic is chosen the leader follows these steps:

1. Locate all references to the topic in a concordance, Bible dictionary, or topical or study Bible. For example, if the group wishes to do a topical study on holiness, a concordance will list all the passages in the Bible in which this word appears. A Bible dictionary would indicate other words in the Bible that are also closely related to this topic and those references might be noted. The Thematic Index in the *Concordance to the Good News Bible* also directs you to a "family" of "related" words.

2. Group the references together, and decide which ones are significant and similar and which might therefore be studied at the same time in one session. Also decide which of the references are relatively minor and might be deleted from the study without distortion of the topic.

3. Select the most important references and place them in some kind of order for study – i.e. chronological, or in the order in which they appear in the Bible, thus studying the references in Exodus and Leviticus before the ones in Hebrews and 1 Peter; or logical, with all those which carry a common idea being studied together; or question-oriented, asking questions about the subject and grouping together for study all the verses which help to answer each question.

4. Determine how many sessions the topic will be studied for, and divide the material into the number of sessions available. For example, holiness might be done in a four week or a six week study. Choose the focus and verses to be studied at each meeting.

5. Prepare a study sheet for each member, or on a large piece of paper list the verses to be studied during each meeting.

Procedure

Announce the focus of the topic for the evening and give everyone a copy of the verses for study. You may want to place people in groups of two, three or four to research a set of verses together, and then have each smaller group report to the larger group what they found.

Basic questions for discussion:

O   What do these verses tell us about our topic? How do they define it, expand it, illustrate it or illuminate it?

O   What things do we need to define or study further to understand these verses? Who can help us with this?

O   How would you summarize what we are learning? What are the most important concepts or exhortations?

O   What can we apply to ourselves from what we learn from these verses? How do they challenge or shape our beliefs? How do they affect our lives?

Keys to success

O   Verses chosen for topical study need to be centrally related to the topic so that their relevance can be seen easily.

O   Tangents are an ever-present danger in topical studies, and the leader needs to be prepared to help the group to stay on the subject.

O   Bible dictionaries are sometimes useful tools to use after the first work on

the appropriate verses has been done by the group. They can help the group to see if the major ideas have been grasped or if other things still need to be studied.
○   Topics should be big enough, or important enough to the faith to warrant this kind of attention.

Resources
Concordance, Topical Bible, Bible dictionary, study guides.
   See the examples of topical studies.

Example 1

Topical Study

Learning to pray from Old Testament personalities

Some of the most important examples and principles of prayer can be found in the Old Testament accounts of the relationship between different people and God. These prayers are worthy of careful study as a means to build up our own prayer life. We can learn from them why people prayed, how they prayed, and what happened when they prayed. Some important prayers are:

Abraham: Genesis 18
Jacob: Genesis 32
Moses: Exodus 3 – 4; Exodus 32
Hannah: 1 Samuel 2
David: Psalm 51 (see 2 Samuel 11); Psalm 139
Solomon: 1 Kings 3; 2 Chronicles 6
Elijah: 1 Kings 19
Elisha: 2 Kings 6.8-23
Hezekiah: 2 Kings 18 – 19
Jehoshaphat: 2 Chronicles 20
Isaiah: Isaiah 6.1-8
Jeremiah: Jeremiah 1.1-10
Jonah: Jonah 2

A suggested method of study: Choose one prayer.

1. Read the passage through to gain an understanding of the historical and personal situation of the person praying. Who is praying and why? Discuss.

2. Outline the prayer. Identify each separate idea expressed. What are the parts of the prayer? What is said to God, about God? About the person or people praying? About the situation? What request is made? What confession? What praise and thanksgiving? Discuss.

3. Ask: What do we learn about God from this prayer? About the person praying? About ourselves and our situation? What parts of this prayer can we pray? Which parts are strange to us? What challenges your faith? How did God answer this prayer? How do we want him to answer us? How will we wait for his answer?

Example 2

Topical Study

Prayers for Christians
in Paul's Letters and the Letter to the Hebrews

1. Ephesians 1.15-23; 3.14-19
2. Philippians 1.3-5, 9-11
3. Colossians 1.3-5, 9-14
4. 1 Thessalonians 1.2-3; 5.23-25
5. 2 Thessalonians 1.11-12; 3.1-2; Philemon 4-6
6. Hebrews 13.20-21

Study and discussion guide: Choose one group of prayers. Read through and discuss one prayer at a time.

1. What is the setting, occasion or context for the prayer? Who is praying for whom?

2. Is anything said about the one being prayed to? What names, titles, or characteristics of God are mentioned and highlighted in the prayer?

3. Is there a statement of thanksgiving? What is the writer thankful for?

4. What requests or petitions are made on behalf of the Christians? List each clause separately. Are there any cause and effect relationships suggested in the prayer? e.g. I ask for . . . so that . . . will be true. What pronouns, conjunctions, adjectives, adverbs, verbs are used?

5. Is there a central or main thought expressed in the prayer? Why did the writer pray this, do you think? Why does he think this is important?

6. Attempt to re-state the requests made in your own words.

Praying the prayer: Application:

1. Write or carefully think your way through the various statements of the prayer, placing yourself in the prayer. What are you thankful for? What characteristics of God mentioned can you rejoice in? How are the needs expressed in the prayer like your needs? How do they challenge your faith and life?

2. Whom do you need to pray for? Go through the prayer, putting in the person or group of people for whom you are concerned. Move each general petition to make it as specific as possible towards the people for whom you are praying, e.g. "Help them to have the knowledge of your will in the decisions being made about . . ." In a time of group prayer, pray for each other, using what you have learned to guide you.

5. WORD STUDY

Preparation

Steps the leader should follow before the meeting:

1. Choose a word for study which is significant and occurs often enough in the Bible to be worth the group's time for study. Look at related forms of the word. For example, freedom, free; salvation, saved, save; ministry, minister; serve, servant.

2. Consult a concordance or topical Bible to locate all the passages where the word occurs. Discover: How often does the word occur and where? Does the word appear to have the same meaning whenever it occurs, or is it used in different ways by different authors?

3. Decide on the key passages for group investigation. **Limit** the amount of material. List the passages the group will investigate.

4. Provide tools for group use like dictionaries, word books and different translations of the Bible.

Procedure

1. The leader announces the word for study and asks each member to write a one or two sentence definition in their own words. This should take three to four minutes.

2. The leader displays, reads or writes out or hands out a list of the key passages where the word occurs, along with dictionaries, word books, the Thematic Index from the *Concordance to the Good News Bible* and/or other translations.

Divide the large group into groups of two, three or four people. Each group should look up each reference in sequence and answer these questions:

How is the word used and what does it mean in this passage? How does the context in which it appears help to define this term?

As we look at each new reference, how does it further illuminate the meaning of this term? Is anything new added or emphasized? Is anything changed? What do our reference tools add to our understanding of our term? What are our conclusions about its meaning? How do these match or expand what we had written in the beginning?

Allow twenty to twenty-five minutes for this step.

3. The groups now have a time of discussion.

Reports: Each small group is asked to report. What did you discover about this word? Why is it important?

General discussion: If you had to explain this word to someone who had no idea of what it meant, how, after your study, and in your own words, would you define it? What is its significance? Why is this word relevant to Christian belief and behaviour?

Allow fifteen to twenty minutes for this step.

Resources

New Testament Words, William Barclay, Westminster Press, 1976.

A Theological Word Book of the Bible, Alan Richardson, Macmillan, 1962.

See the example of the word study on "Grace".

Example

Word Study: "Grace"

Key passages:

John 1.14-16
Romans 3.21-25; 5.1-2; 6.1-2, 15-23
2 Corinthians 12.7-10
Ephesians 1.5-10; 2.4-10

Colossians 1.2-8
2 Timothy 2.1
2 Peter 3.18

Extracts from the definition of grace in the *Oxford Concise Dictionary:*

7. Unconstrained goodwill as ground of concession.

9. Unmerited favour of God, divine regenerating, inspiring, and strengthening influence; divinely given talent etc.

11. Mercy, clemency.

12. Short thanksgiving before or after meal.

Study and discussion guide:

1. Study each passage to discover the context of the word "grace" and how it is used. To whom or what does it refer? What does it mean in the setting of each passage?

2. In your own contemporary language, how would you define or describe "grace"? Are there different uses of the term? Are there different aspects of grace? If so, what?

3. Read the dictionary definition of the term. Is it adequate? Accurate?

4. Why is grace such an important and much used word in the New Testament?

5. Based upon your study, what is our relationship to grace? How is grace received? How can it be abused? What is its purpose in our lives? How do we "grow in grace"?

6. BIOGRAPHICAL STUDY

Preparation

1. Choose the person to be studied. Biblical characters on which there is sufficient material for studies of three to six weeks include:

Abraham	Samuel	Jonah
Jacob	Saul	Daniel
Joseph	David	Mary the mother of Jesus
Moses	Elijah	Peter
Ruth	Nehemiah	Paul

Brief studies of one to three weeks could be done on:

Sarah	Hannah	James and John
Hagar	Naaman	Zacchaeus
Miriam	Hezekiah	Mary Magdalene
Joshua	Mary and Martha	Barnabas
Deborah		

2. Locate all the biblical references to this person using a concordance or a reference Bible. Decide how to divide up the material for each of the available study times.

Procedure

Personal study: Get the group to read the assigned reference to the person, asking: What do you learn about the person?

Group discussion: Choose some of these questions for discussion.

O   What are the basic facts about our person, family, job, economic situation, roles, responsibilities?

O   What are the key relationships in this person's life, and how are they handled?

O   What happens to this person, and how do they respond?

O   What feelings are present in this life and why?

O   What struggles or conflicts did he or she experience? Why did they emerge? How were they resolved?

O   What do you learn about this person's faith in God? Does it change, grow or develop? Or does it deteriorate? Why?

O   Put yourself in this person's position. Can you identify with anything in them or in their situation? What? How?

O   What can we learn from this person to apply to our own lives?

Keys to success

O   Move below the surface of the biographical details, using your imagination to re-create the setting and feelings of the story.

O   Encourage personal responses: Is this person's experience like anything you have seen or experienced? How?

O   Push towards lessons that can be drawn. Ask: Why do you think the story of this person has been preserved for so many years? What does it have to teach us?

Resource

Bible dictionary or encyclopedia.

6

More Bible Study Methods in Small Groups

When your group wants to emphasize personal interaction or appropriation of the Scriptures, the following methods should be considered. Many of them can be completed in relatively brief time periods. They are suitable either for groups with extensive biblical background or for groups which do not have the time or inclination for more lengthy and disciplined methods of systematic Bible study. Some require serious commitment and involve an intense interaction with the Scriptures and with other group members. When choosing appropriate methods you should consider the experiences, abilities, and interests of group members as well as the group contract.

Set Two: Methods focused on Response

Some people benefit from an approach to Bible study which focuses on intellectual discovery and understanding. They focus on gaining a grasp of the content of Scripture in order to know and understand its message. Others prefer a method which relates more to life, moving beyond concepts and generalized statements to experiential involvement with the text. These methods require more personal interaction with the text and hold a promise of a discussion which moves rapidly to personal reaction and application.

7. DEVOTIONAL STUDY: READING, REFLECTION AND READING

Preparation

Choose a passage of Scripture which does not require extensive background or explanation. Biblical narratives, stories from the Gospels, and key paragraphs from the shorter letters of Paul, James, Peter and John, are especially suitable.

Procedure

1. Ask the group to read the selected passage in silence and then ask one member of the group to read it aloud. You might want to spend a few moments praying aloud or silently. Then spend a few moments in silence, allowing each member to re-read and reflect on the passage with one " question for reflection". Some may wish to write their reactions to the passage. Sample questions include:

What do I learn from this passage? How does this passage encourage, threaten or challenge me? What feelings are present in the passage, and what feelings are triggered in me as I read it? What does this passage say, and what does it say to me? How does this story "speak to my condition"? What does this passage teach me about God and myself? Where am I in this story, and where do I want to be? What speaks to me in this passage? What issues does this passage raise that are important to life? What does this passage teach, and what can I learn from it?

2. After a few moments of silence, ask for one person to share aloud his or her answer to the question that has been asked. Then ask others for their answers or reactions to the passage. Group members may ask the person sharing to say more or to explain something, but there should be no debate or attempt to achieve a group consensus about a particular point. After everyone has shared their responses, the leader then shares his or her own response to the text. The time may end with one more reading aloud of the text (if it is b with one more reading aloud of the text (if it is brief), or the group may move to a time of personal sharing of concerns and needs or prayer.

Advantages

O   This method requires almost no preparation and allows for great freedom to respond to a given text.

O   Sometimes people can gain great insights and have very real experiences as a result of silence and reflection.

O   Hearing how others respond to the text may sharpen and challenge one's own response.

O   Sympathetic understanding between group members will grow if group members learn to listen carefully to each other and respond positively to thoughts and ideas that are shared.

Keys to success

O   The time of silence must not be rushed, yet it should not be so long that people feel a vacuum and become restless. Many people fear silence in groups and do not know how to use the time profitably, so three to five minutes of silence may be the maximum possible for a group that is just beginning. More mature groups can handle longer times with great profit. If there are only one or two minutes of silence, the sharing may be shallow and superficial.

O   A few preliminary comments, very brief lest they become a sermon, may help avoid mistakes in understanding the text, otherwise there is the danger of misinterpreting the passage because group members do not have the information they need to understand the text.

8. PARAPHRASING AND RESPONSE

Preparation

If the group regularly uses non-paraphrased versions of the Bible (like the *Authorized Version, Revised Standard Version, New English Bible, New International Version,* or *Good News Bible*), and wants to study non-narrative material, then this method is helpful. Choose a section of Scripture like 1 Corinthians 13 or other sections from Paul's letters to the Corinthians, Romans, etc. Block the section into paragraphs if this is not already done in the printed text. Have paper and pens or pencils as well as a copy of the text available for each group member. Choose one or two paragraphs for the group to work on, probably no more than six verses at a time.

Procedure

1. If they do not have their own, give each person paper and a pen and a copy of the text divided into paragraphs. Ask each one to read the text in silence, and then to rewrite or translate the first verse of the key paragraph in their own words, trying to put it into ordinary everyday language. Allow three to four minutes.

2. Stop and ask two or three people to share what they have written. The leader should say something positive about each effort, especially commenting on the way in which someone was able to find the meaning in the verse and re-state it in his or her own words.

3. Ask people to continue with the rest of the passage, writing their own paraphrases of each verse. Allow ten to fifteen minutes for this.

4. Call "Time" and ask people to go back and re-read silently what they have written. Ask them to pick out one thing that they would like to do something about or work on in their own lives. Ask them to write one or two sentences about this application of the passage, being sure to include something about what they could do to act on this during the coming week.

5. Here the leader must decide whether to keep the whole group together for sharing, or whether to break it up into groups of four. In the smaller group everyone has an opportunity to share in some depth, and it only takes about fifteen minutes. If the whole group stays together, not everyone will be able to share their paraphrase because of the time this would take.

Ask for each (or some) to share his or her paraphrase. Ask group members to listen carefully and to be prepared to ask one question of the person sharing. When the person finishes sharing his or her paraphrase, ask one or two people (different ones each time) if they have a question they wish to ask. These questions may ask for an illustration or explanation or might ask more directly, for example: Do you think what Paul is saying is really possible in everyday life today? Or: What do you feel about what is being suggested? The leader should help the discussion not to be theoretical. Also one person should not be allowed to take too much time. Try to get as many paraphrases shared as the time permits. Spend about thirty minutes.

6. After a number of paraphrases have been shared and discussed, ask each person to share what they wrote down for application, with any brief explanation they want to add. Do not discuss these, but move fairly quickly so each has time to contribute. The simplest procedure is to move around the circle, with the leader going first so as to set the tone. Be as personal, practical and honest as possible.

7. End the sharing time with a time of group prayer, praying by name for each other and for the things that have been shared. You may want to end the prayer time with members holding hands and praying together the Lord's Prayer.

Resources

Lyman Coleman has written many small group resource books suitable for teenagers and adults, with numerous suggestions and helpful materials which can be used as written or adapted for use in different settings. The preceding steps have been adapted from his recommendations. For a more complete description see *Search the Scripture*.

9. EXPLORING PERSONAL PROBLEMS IN THE LIGHT OF SCRIPTURE

Suitability

When a number of members in a group are experiencing, or can expect to experience, common struggles and difficulties, the group may want to do topical studies focused on biblical material helpful in working through these issues.

Some problems and possible passages for study are:

Forgiveness: Luke 23.32-34; Ephesians 4.17-32 (especially 31-32); Matthew 6.7-15; John 18.15-18, 25-27 and 21.1-19.

Broken relationships and conflicts: Jacob and Esau, Genesis 25 – 33; Matthew 5.21-26; John 15 – 17; 1 Corinthians 1.10-17; Philippians 2.1-11.

Worry: Matthew 6.25-34; Philippians 4.6-9.

Depression: Elijah, 1 Kings 18 – 19.

Unanswered prayer: Luke 11.1-13, 18.1-14; James 1.5-8, 4.1-10, 5.13-18; 2 Corinthians 12.7-10; 1 John 5.13-15.

Marital difficulties: Ephesians 5.21-33; 1 Corinthians 7.1-17; 1 Corinthians 13; 1 Peter 3.1-7.

Differences in the Christian community: 1 Corinthians 12; Philippians 2.1-11; 2 Timothy 2.14-26.

Discouragement and a lack of joy: Philippians; John 15.1-11; 2 Corinthians 1.3-11; Psalm 23, 150.

Hostility and rejection from non-Christians: Matthew 5.1-16; Acts 4; 2 Timothy 1.8-18; Hebrews 12.1-14; Revelation 2 – 3.
Suffering: 1 Peter 1.3-9, 2.18-25; James 1.2-4, 5.7-11; Isaiah 53.
Temptation: Luke 4.1-13; 1 Corinthians 10.12-13; Hebrews 2.14-18.

Preparation

1. Through prayer and awareness of the needs and situations of members of the group, the leader, perhaps in discussion with a few or all of the group members, chooses the problem and biblical materials to focus upon. Only one problem should be discussed in a meeting.

Warning Not all personal problems have biblical materials which bear directly upon the central issue. For this reason, the leader who is aware of problems with which group members wrestle will want to choose a topic which does have enough biblical material, and which has enough general relevance to all the group members to warrant group time and examination. Problems which are less focused, more diffused or very personal to just one group member may be shared for prayer but should not be chosen for this kind of study.

Using a topical Bible, a subject or thematic index, or a concordance, the leader (or group members) searches for passages which seem related to the problem chosen for discussion. These questions may aid in the search:

O   Did anyone in the Bible experience a similar problem? Who? When? Where is their story told and what can we learn from it?

O   Is this problem mentioned by Jesus in any of his parables or in his teaching? Did Jesus ever experience this difficulty? What can we learn from him?

O   Did the early Christians ever experience this problem? Where is it described? What did they do and what suggestions might we draw from their experiences?

O   Is there any systematic instruction about this problem in the New Testament? Are there key words we could look up in a concordance to locate this teaching?

O   If there are many examples, or many passages on this subject, which ones are the closest to our own situation or the most helpful for group study?

After searching the Scriptures, select the one or two key stories or passages for group study.

2. An introductory question related to the problem should be developed. These questions may help you in thinking through the problem to develop this "springboard" question:

What is the problem? What is the "dis-ease" being experienced or likely to be experienced? What is the setting or situation within which the problem commonly occurs? What are the feelings that accompany the problem? How strong or upsetting are they? Are there non-group members involved in the problem? How do they affect the situation? What are the needs of the people in the group? How do group members experience and work with this problem? Is there a key word that will help members get in touch with their ideas and feelings about this subject?

3. Develop a "springboard question", such as:

When, if ever, have you struggled with depression, and what did it feel like? Have you ever suffered for your faith as a Christian? What happened and how did you cope with it? Think of a time when you were in conflict with another person and you couldn't seem to solve it. What did you feel at that time, and how did the conflict affect you? Has anyone here ever had trouble forgiving someone for something? What made it so hard? Have you ever prayed seriously for something and felt that God wasn't answering? How did it affect you? Is there one struggle you've had in your married life that you wouldn't mind sharing with the group? How did you feel while you were going through it?

Procedure
1. Exploring the problem
The leader asks the springboard question. When people begin to respond, the leader extends the discussion by asking others to share their experiences, either personal experiences or ones they have seen in others who struggle with this problem. Try to move beyond theoretical discussion to get at feelings: How did you (or they) feel about that? Or personal relevance: Is this something you have ever struggled with? Or general relevance: How often does this problem occur, do you think? Where and when is it likely to occur?

The goal at this stage is to bring the problem to the surface and define it with enough clarity so that all the group members know what is involved. A description of the problem itself, the accompanying feelings, and any contributing people or factors is what is desired. Since you are not seeking a specific solution to the problem, time should be limited and focused upon clarity and shared understanding. Key skills required include active listening to the person or people sharing their ideas and feelings, and asking questions for clarification. Allow five to twenty-five minutes for this stage.

2. Searching the Scriptures
The leader announces that the group will now look at one or more biblical passages which are related to the problem we have been discussing. Give the members time to find the passage and then ask one member to read it aloud if it is relatively brief. If you are studying several chapters, announce the chapters and give five to ten minutes for reading. Ask group members to read the selected materials looking for events, experiences, or instructions related to the problem being discussed. Then ask one or two observation questions – e.g. who are the characters in this story and what happens to them? Or, what does this passage say and how is it related to our topic? Then discuss the key event or main idea in the passage as it relates to the topic.
Key question What was the experience or counsel of the person or the writer and what can we learn from this about the problem at hand? Why was it written? What is the central thrust of the story? What is the passage teaching us? Spend at least twenty-five to thirty minutes in a careful examination of the facts, feelings, events, key concepts, and applicability of the passage.

3. Personal application
After a good discussion of the biblical material, the leader asks the group to spend some moments reflecting on the question: When, if ever, is the problem that we have been discussing a problem for you, or a problem for those you care about? What help do you need to meet the problem or challenge for yourself or others? What resources are available? This reflection may be done in silence, in writing, or in general group discussion. Give at least ten to fifteen minutes to this step before moving to prayer.

Keys to success

O Do not let the discussion become focused on one person's problem and how to solve it. Focus instead on a more general discussion of the subject and of the ways different people meet and deal with it. This is not a problem-solving meeting but a discussion of a problem common to many Christians with a look at biblical materials to gain insight and perspective.

O Avoid "advice-giving" and focus on general principles and positive possibilities. The value in a study like this can be in the encouragement that comes from knowing one is not alone in having problems and that there is help which can be gained from Scripture and the Christian community.

O Always end the discussion in prayer, committing any needs to the Lord and expressing gratitude for his willingness to hear and answer.

10. RELATIONAL BIBLE STUDY (DEALING WITH THE DISCOVERY AND BUILDING OF RELATIONSHIPS)

This method focuses upon four basic relationships as it looks at biblical materials: our relationship to God, our relationship to ourselves, our relationship to other people, our relationship to the world.

Preparation

Choose a story from the Bible which is brief and self-contained. Stories Jesus told and stories of Jesus' interaction with people are especially appropriate. Good examples would include the story of the prodigal son and the elder brother (Luke 15.11-32), Peter and the catch of fish (Luke 5.1-11), Jesus with Mary, Martha, and Lazarus (John 11), Jesus with Simon and the sinful woman (Luke 7.36-50), the story of the banquet (Luke 14.7-24), the story of the Good Samaritan (Luke 10.25-37), etc.

Procedure

1. Ask someone to read the story aloud. Then ask group members to read it through silently and carefully, asking this question: What are the personal relationships that exist in this passage? After a few moments, call "Time" and ask the question of the group in general. Spend five to eight minutes identifying these relationships.

2. After general discussion, the leader says: There are four key relationships that all of us experience: our relationship to God, our relationship to ourselves, our relationship to other people, and our relationship to the world. The quality and character of these relationships shape who we are and how we live our lives. From this passage, how do the people in this story experience these relationships, and what was important to them? What was positive or negative in their relationships? Who initiates or changes the relationship? What can we learn about one or more of these four key relationships? Give each person a chance to share.

3. Ask one of the following questions for general discussion: What does this story show you about one of your key relationships? . . . about your relationship to God? . . . to yourself? . . . to others? . . . to the world? What can you discover in this story that could lead to greater personal wholeness? Finally ask: What steps, if any, would you want to take to improve or strengthen one of these four relationships in your life? How might you begin?

Key to success

○   Whenever the discussion seems too general, abstract or irrelevant, ask a question such as: Is this something you have experienced or struggled with? When? How? How does this principle (issue, statement, idea, proposition) work out in your life? What difference does this make for us, in our lives?

Set Three: Methods focused on Encounter

The next group of methods tend to move somewhat deeper into the text and into personal encounter. Some may find these methods too personal or too demanding for comfort. Others will welcome the opportunity for an in-depth encounter with the text and with other members of the group. These methods presuppose a willingness for self-disclosure and some risk-taking, along with a serious commitment to wrestling with the text and its personal and corporate applications.

11. FEELINGS AND FAITH: ENCOUNTER WITH THE PSALMS

Preparation

One of the "feeling-laden" psalms is chosen which deals with experiences and feelings likely to be known to group members. Examples: Psalm 32, 38, 51, 55, 56, 71, 73, 77, 139, 143, 147, etc. Identify both the negative and positive feelings being expressed by the psalmist. Divide the psalm into major paragraphs or blocks of similar material.

Procedure

1. Announce the psalm to be used for "encounter". Ask the group to read the psalm in silence, looking for the feelings that are present. Then ask the group members to read the psalm aloud in unison with as much feeling in their voices as they can muster. Or have the psalm read aloud antiphonally, with one member reading one verse and the other group members reading the alternate verses. Or, if any group members are willing and able, ask them to prepare in advance, and then have the psalm read aloud while one or more group members dance or move in such a way as to display the feelings present in the psalm.

2. Ask members for one-word statements to express the experiences and feelings present in the psalm. Do not discuss these or allow sentences or long phrases. Encourage each person to say one or two words which capture a feeling in the psalm or in their response to the psalm. Then ask: What are the feelings present in the first major section, and why do you think the psalmist feels this way? Move to the next major block of material and ask: Do you see any change in feelings here or later in this psalm? If so, what and why? What causes the change? Discuss each major section of the psalm. Additional questions might include: How intense are the feelings present? What prayer does the psalmist pray? What encourages or discourages the writer? What does his faith mean to him?

3. Ask: When, if ever, has anyone here felt like the psalmist? What triggered it off? What was it like? What encouraged or discouraged you at that time? Has anyone else ever felt like this? Allow for as many to share as would like to. Then ask: Is anyone experiencing any of these things in your life at the present time? How intensely? What discourages you and what encourages you in this

situation? Allow extensive time for personal sharing if people open up and want to talk. Do not allow criticism or "advice-giving". Listen intently and encourage others to listen carefully to what is being shared. Do not rush.

4. If time remains, the leader may wish to ask: Did the psalmist experience any resolution? Any hope? How did it come? Would one or more of you share – what resolution do you hope for? How might it come to you? What signs of hope can you see?

5. Writing your own psalm. Consider ending with a time of silence, inviting members to re-read the psalm, or to write a psalm of their own which expresses their concerns, feelings and prayers. Allow five to seven minutes for this. If psalms are written, invite people to share them with the other members of the group as part of the closing prayer.

Keys to success

O   Ask the fewest possible questions to help members explore the feelings of the psalmist and their own feelings.

O   Avoid generalizations such as "many people experience . . ." and "lots of people think . . ." in order to focus concretely and specifically on the psalm and the people in the group. Ask instead: What do you feel? What do you think? If strong feelings are shared and some helpful response is needed, consider gathering in a circle around the member expressing the need, and praying for him or her. Then resume your places and discussion as appropriate.

12. DEPTH AND ENCOUNTER

This is a method which combines several of the methods described earlier.

Preparation

Choose passages of Scripture which lend themselves to paraphrasing and speak to central aspects of the Christian life. John Mallison in *Creative Ideas for Small Groups in the Christian Community* suggests some of the following possibilities:

Romans 8.1-19; 12.1-2 Hebrews 12.1-17
Ephesians 3.16-19 1 John 1; 2.9-11
Philippians 1.27-30; 2.1-13; 4.4-13 Matthew 5.3-16
2 Timothy 2.1-5, 14-15 John 15.9-21, 26-27

Procedure

1. Announce the passage, and ask each person to write out their own paraphrase or translation of the passage verse by verse in their own words, as if they were writing to a friend. After sufficient time has been given for this task (ten to fifteen minutes), ask each one to take a few moments and reflect on the passage they have just translated using this question: What would happen if I took this seriously? Allow about five minutes for this stage. Members may write a response if they wish.

2. Form into small groups of up to four or five people. Take turns asking each person to read their translation and share their answer to the questions: What would happen if I took this seriously? What difference would it make? Group

members may ask the one who is sharing for explanation or for more details, attempting to stay concrete and application-oriented in the discussion. An additional step to aid in good listening is to ask one member to attempt to re-state what they heard from another member's sharing. The original speaker is then given an opportunity to correct, clarify or add to what they said. Take between twenty and thirty minutes for this sharing. Whenever the discussion becomes theoretical or too general, someone should ask a question like: How would that affect your (our) lives? Or: So what? What real difference does it make? Or: What is the personal implication of what you are saying? How does this matter in your situation? Or: What are we (you) to do as a result of this? Or: Does this suggest any need for change? How will this change come about?

3. Re-assemble as a large group. Ask if anyone would like to share their translations or applications with the whole group. Allow several to share. Ask if anyone would like to share anything from their discussion in the smaller groups for the larger group to consider. Allow time for sharing and some discussion. Finally, ask: What challenges or impresses you most deeply from this passage or from our discussion? Close with a time of silence and prayer.

13. TRANSFORMATIONAL BIBLE STUDY

In some ways this can be the most simple and the most difficult of all methods of Bible study. Taking 2 Timothy 3.16 as the key assumption, that "All scripture . . . is useful for teaching the truth, rebuking error, correcting faults, and giving instruction for right living . . ." this method asks four key questions of any passage:

1. What truth does this passage teach? (What should I/we believe?)
2. How does the passage reveal and rebuke error? (What should I/we reject?)
3. What can be learned from this passage to help correct faults and put things right? (How can I/we change?)
4. What instructions does this passage give to direct our (my) living? (How should I/we behave?)

All these questions cannot be answered from every passage, but asking and answering these questions about a passage can help in that process of transformation and renewal of the mind of which the apostle Paul speaks in Romans 12.1-2.

Preparation

Choose a book of the Bible or key chapters for group study over a period of six to twelve weeks, for example Ephesians or Colossians. The leader should study the passage in advance using the four key questions as a guide. Decide which of the questions are most useful or if one or more should be omitted as unhelpful in this specific instance.

Procedure

1. Announce the passage for study and remind the group of the four key questions. Ask someone to read the passage aloud while the others follow in their Bibles. Then ask question 1. Allow a few moments for people to re-read the passage and think about the question, and then call for their response. After the first response, ask: Is there anything else? Keep probing until all have had an opportunity to respond. If responses come which seem inappropriate, don't

correct them yourself as the leader. Ask: What do others of you think about that? Allow the group to interact freely. Before the discussion comes to a complete halt, ask question 2. Discuss. Then question 3 and discuss, and then question 4.

2. After discussing each of the key questions, ask: What do we need to do this week to put this passage into practice? Further questions might include: What is easy and what is hard about doing what this passage calls for? What changes in our beliefs and behaviour does this passage show us we should make? What will each of us do this week because of this scripture? Ask each person who is willing to express one definite thing they intend to do as a result of what the scripture says. Pray together for God's help for the coming week.

3. At the next meeting, do not begin by studying a new passage. Ask: How have you lived out what you learned from Scripture during this past week? Where have you found it helpful? Are you doing it? What has happened?

If most of the group members have found it difficult to apply the passage during the week, the group may want to study the same passage again. If some progress has been made, the passage and principles learned from the previous week may be reviewed before going on to the next passage. The group leader must be prayerfully sensitive to the needs and situations of the group members in making the decision about whether to go forward in the study or to re-study last week's material. If re-study is called for, then use the four key questions again and ask each time: What keeps us from doing this? What help do we need to be able to live this? How can we help each other to do this? The leader must be honest about his or her own efforts to live the passage, and should not assume a superior attitude.

Keys to success

O   This method assumes a definite willingness on the part of group members to place their lives in submission to God by taking very seriously what is learned from Scripture in fellowship with other Christians. Often we "know" much more than we live. If we slow down our pace of study in order to concentrate on "learning to live" from the Bible, instead of rushing on to study new verses in the Bible, our lack of serious discipleship may be revealed, as well as the very real problems which Christians encounter. The desire in this method is not to "know" more but to be transformed from within as our lives are submitted to God and to each other as we encounter the Scriptures. This assumes that the Bible study is not over when the group finishes meeting, but that the Bible shapes belief and behaviour between meetings as well.

O   Patience, love, careful listening, and mutual forgiveness are necessary ingredients for this method to work. The leader, especially, must be as positive as possible, offering encouragement and affirmation while calling the group to serious effort to live what is being learned.

O   Group members must have agreed to the purposes of this method or they will not be able to handle the frustrations and failures which accompany any serious attempt to follow Christ. This method does, when taken seriously, allow for personal life change which, when shared with other group members, builds joy and faith.

14. YOU ARE THERE: ROLE-PLAYING AND DRAMATIZATION

Preparation

Choose a section of Scripture, either Old or New Testament, which lends itself to dramatization. Choose stories which include conflict and action, usually with more than two characters. Examples include the story of the woman taken in adultery (John 8.1-11), Peter and John and the lame man (Acts 3 – 4), Paul and Silas and the Philippian jailer (Acts 16.16-40), Jesus, the disciples and the storm (Luke 8.22-25), David, Uriah, Bathsheba, and Nathan (2 Samuel 11-12), the prodigal son, the father and the elder brother (Luke 15.11-32), etc.

Identify all the characters and groups of people present in the story.

Before the group meeting, you may wish to assign parts to several of the group members and ask them to read the whole story through in advance and come prepared to read or re-enact the story as one of the characters.

Procedure

1. Introduce the story. Several approaches might be used. One way is to announce the story, assign parts to all the group members (assigning more than one person to play each character) and give them ten to fifteen minutes to read, discuss their part in groups of two or three, and decide how they would like to present their character in the re-enactment of the story. After ten minutes or so, call "Time" and ask them to present the story. Or, have group members listen as the story is told or enacted by those who have prepared before the meeting. Ask: What are your first impressions as you hear this story? Allow five to fifteen minutes for discussion.

2. Ask all the group members to choose one character with whom to identify as they read the story, trying to imagine themselves in the scene. Check and see if every character or group of characters has been chosen. If not, assign this character to someone. Each should ask himself: What am I seeing, feeling, thinking, doing as a participant in this story? If you are using a Gospel story, suggest that they choose some character other than Jesus with whom to identify, at least at first. If there is enough time, group members can be asked to identify with more than one character.

3. After reading and reflection, ask: With whom did you identify in this story and why? Discuss each character or group in the order in which they appear in the story. As each character is mentioned ask: What do you think is happening to and inside this character? Why did they behave as they did at each stage in the story? What are their actions and reactions? What do you learn from the perspective of this person? Give each person in the group a chance to share in answering at least one of these questions.

4. If time permits, consider discussing: Who in this story are you most like? Least like? Who would you like to be like? Why? How?

5. Discuss: What can we learn from this story?

Resource

Using the Bible in Drama by Steve and Janet Stickley and Jim Belben.

15. KNOWING GOD AND OURSELVES: MEDITATION

This is a method of guided individual meditation which may or may not be shared with fellow group members at its conclusion. Group members must know each other well enough and feel comfortable enough with each other to be able to sit in silence, meditating on Scripture while the others around are doing the same.

Preparation
Choose a section of Scripture suitable for meditation. Psalms are especially good for beginners. Gospel materials on the last week of Jesus' life, including the Upper Room discourses in John 13 – 17, are also very helpful. You may wish to prepare two or three questions or instructions for how to meditate, and reproduce them so that each member may have a copy.

Procedure
1. The leader directs the group members to close their eyes and begin a process of centring. In this process they are asked to relax physically, perhaps by tensing and releasing certain muscles like those in the legs, hands, and face, and mentally by releasing all cares and concerns to a loving heavenly Father who knows and cares for them. (See *Celebration of Discipline* by Richard Foster for practical help with this.)

In the silence they are then invited to focus on the loving presence of God and to pray inwardly prayers of adoration and gratitude. A single verse may be said to help in this process, such as "Give thanks to the LORD, because he is good; his love is eternal." (Psalm 107.1) "Thanks be to God who gives us the victory through our Lord Jesus Christ." (1 Corinthians 15.57) "Leave all your worries with him, because he cares for you." (1 Peter 5.7) "Where two or three come together in my name, I am there with them." (Matthew 18.20) Close this section with the Lord's Prayer or an Amen.

2. Announce the Scripture for meditation. Psalm 1 is a good place to begin. Tell members how many minutes they have to enjoy the silence and to meditate on the psalm. A group which is just beginning may take ten minutes. More advanced groups could use thirty to sixty minutes.

As a focus for meditation, they may wish to read the psalm through slowly a few times, paying attention to images and ideas which emerge. They may wish to write out the psalm slowly, seeking to reflect on each key word or phrase as they write; they may wish to ask: What does God want to say to me through this part of his Word? They may wish to write down their thoughts on the psalm, noting whatever emerges from careful attention to the psalm and the self. They may wish to explore feelings, ideas, disturbing elements aroused by the psalm. They may use the question: What does this psalm tell me about God and about myself? The key idea is to slow down, silence the distractions externally and internally, and allow the psalm or Scripture to speak to the self in the silence.

3. A minute or two before concluding the time of silence, tell the members that there are only two or three minutes left if they wish to note anything or finish off what they are doing. Then after the time, gather together and ask if anyone has anything that they wish to share with the others. Wait a few moments. If no one speaks, move to the closing prayer. If someone shares, ask when they have finished if anyone else would like to share anything. Do not encourage a general discussion but allow for personal sharing one by one.

Keys to success
O   Eliminate distractions from noise or people as much as possible. If a garden

or a large room is available and the weather is suitable, you may wish to encourage people to move apart to various places for the time of meditation.
O   Paper, pens and copies of the text should be available.
O   Questions written for meditation and given to each member in writing may help them to focus and make the best use of their time.
O   Give clear instructions so that people know how long the time will be, what is expected of them and how they might proceed. Most Christians today have very little experience with meditation and the regular use of solitude as a spiritual discipline. A directed experience in a group can teach members how to do this, so that they can meditate at home and in other settings. It can also become a very powerful group experience if a sense of God is experienced and shared.

16. SING A JOYFUL SONG: SINGING OR LISTENING, WRITING OR PLAYING

Christian faith has always been a singing faith. Much of Scripture has been put to song. Whether in classical hymn, gospel song or more contemporary music, it is possible to find a great deal of Scripture set to music. Some in our groups may have musical gifts and will find great satisfaction in helping to set Scripture to music, or in composing songs based upon Scripture, or in helping group members to sing their faith. Many recordings of music drawn from Scripture are now available, from Handel's *Messiah* to songs by the most recent Christian singing group. Using music, for some groups, will take a bit of time and planning, but the benefits can be enormous.

Preparation

Think and pray about the gifts and inclinations of group members, then make a decision about what kind of musical involvement would be most helpful and appropriate. If all of them hate singing, then a thirty minute singing time could be most embarrassing.

After choosing whether to listen to, sing or compose music, find the resources you will need. If you have been studying a particular passage of Scripture, you may want to search for hymns and songs based on it. Church hymnbooks and collections of more recent songs could be bought or borrowed. If a group is to sing, it is important that everyone can see a copy of the words so that everyone may join in. If a musical instrument would be helpful, arrange for someone to come and play it. If you can't carry a tune yourself, arrange for one of the other members of the group to be the song leader. If you plan to play a piece of recorded music, make sure before the meeting that the machine is there and working. If anything can break, it usually will. Check the record or tape and equipment carefully, so that group members' time is not wasted during the meeting.

Procedure

Make a joyful noise unto the Lord! Don't worry about perfection or professionalism. Say a few positive words about music and faith, give out the song books and begin. Don't assume everyone knows the song being suggested. Spend some moments calling attention to the words and their significance, particularly in second and third verses. If there are any difficult parts in the tune, or if the tune is completely new to some people, get one or two who do know it to sing it for the others, before asking everyone to join in. Do not sing just to fill time. Sing as a means of worshipping God and expressing your faith to others. It is better to sing one or two songs well, with understanding and commitment, than to sing at length without attention and sincerity. Always make certain that newcomers are given songbooks and helped to find what is being sung.

If someone has written a song, the group may want to read the passage upon which the song is based before listening. If music is to be listened to, members should be told what is to be played and anything special that they should listen for.

Many people will remember Scripture that they have sung, long after they have forgotten what they have read. Music is a powerful tool for expression, teaching and helping people to remember.

17. PREPARING FOR ACTION

Set Four: Methods focused on Action

When a group has as its purpose the tackling of a need or problem in the church or in the world, it usually needs to begin with a programme of study. Action without a proper foundation of information and understanding will be ineffective, and perhaps even harmful or counter-productive. The study which is needed is usually two-fold: First the study of the problem or situation itself, to understand its causes, dimensions, characteristics, and possible remedies; and secondly the study of appropriate biblical materials related to the problem at hand.

Some of the suggestions and material listed under method four "Thematic or topical study" (see page 69) would be helpful in this kind of group. Some common problems or needs around which an action or ministry group may form include hunger and poverty, evangelism, injustice and discrimination, peace-making in the nuclear age, strengthening marriages, care for neglected children, helping the unemployed, dealing with minorities, helping the handicapped, caring for the aged, industrial relations, prison ministries, etc.

Preparation

1. When a group knows that it desires to be a "ministry group" or "action group" related to a particular task which needs to be done in the world or the church, decide how many weeks will be allotted to the study phase of the group. If too much time is taken for study, action may never result. If too little time is taken, the action may be useless or wasted. Usually at least three weeks are needed for study, and for some larger issues and problems four to eight weeks would be necessary.

Decide how much of the study time can be devoted to Scripture and how much time to direct study of the particular problem or situation. Usually about one-third of the study time will be spent on Scripture and two-thirds trying to understand the actual need as it exists now. In a ten week action group on hunger, for example, about two weeks might be given to a study of scriptural materials related to this issue; three to four weeks might be given to a study of hunger in your neighbourhood, country, or the world; and the last four or five weeks might be given to strategies for action such as how to increase one's giving to hunger

90

causes, how to work to reduce poverty and hunger in a personal way, how to join with others to meet the needs of the hungry in both short-term and long-term ways.

2. Having decided how much time can be given to the study of the Scriptures, locate relevant passages. Matthew 25.31-46 and Luke 4.14-30 can be considered. Find Christian books on the particular topic in a library or bookshop and see if these are helpful.

One problem is knowing how to find the relevant passages. For instance, looking up all the verses on hunger in a concordance or Bible dictionary can be the place to start, but it will not give you all the relevant passages. A further step is to think through to see that hunger, for instance, is an example of poverty. It is the poor who are hungry. Then do a biblical search for the passages on God's view of the poor, and what are the responsibilities of his people towards the poor. If your "ministry group" or "action group" is focused on evangelism, you should look up all the related passages on the telling of the good news, declaring what God has done, going and making disciples, etc.

3. Choose the particular passages to be studied by the group and the method of approach to use. Almost all the previous methods described could be used.

Procedure

Lead the Bible study using the method chosen. At some point in the study ask one additional question: How should this passage inform or influence our action as individuals and as a group? Ask someone to note down the suggestions that are made, so that they will be available for the discussion about what action to adopt during future group meetings.

18. CURRENT EVENTS AND CHRISTIAN ACTION

It has been suggested that every Christian ought to face the world with the Bible in one hand and the newspaper in the other. This method is a good exercise for a group which tends to focus on its own life and faith to the exclusion of the outside world.

Preparation

Find enough copies of newspapers so that every member can have at least one full page of news.

Procedure

1. Distribute newspapers, and tell members to scan individually or in groups of two at least one page of the paper, looking for two kinds of items. The first item is to be any article or advertisement which has Christian implications, and the second item is to be anything which calls for Christian action. Assure them that there are such items on their page. When they have located their items, ask them in groups of two to brainstorm every possible connection between Christianity and their first item making brief notes so they don't forget, and then to develop a list of every possible action that could be taken in response to their second item. Watch carefully and call "Time" when people seem to have little left to say to each other.

2. Ask members to share their first items and what the relationship is between their item and Christianity. After each one, ask the whole group: Does anyone

see any other relationships between this item and Christianity? Keep the discussion moving at a lively pace.

3. Ask members to share their second item and their list of all possible Christian actions that could be taken in response to that item. After each one, ask: Can anyone think of any other actions that might be taken in response to this? If no one answers, wait a moment and then move on to the next item. Make sure everyone has a chance to share their discoveries.

4. Ask: What, if anything, does this exercise reveal about the relationship between Christian faith and the world as reflected in the newspaper? Then, ask: What, if anything, would anyone like to do as a Christian this week as a result of our discussion?

Keys to success

O   It helps if the leader has done this exercise in advance using the news-papers which will be distributed to the group. He or she can then move around talking quietly to the individuals or groups of two during the work-time and make suggestions if anyone seems stuck.

O   The necessary perspective comes with the affirmation that "Jesus Christ is Lord" and there is nothing that exists that is not related to God and his purposes for the whole created order. Common themes which emerge may relate to the biblical themes of man and woman created in the image of God, sin, reconciliation, covenant, the future of the world, community, forgiveness, work, etc.

19. PRACTISING ACCOUNTABILITY: "DOING THE WORD"

In "Accountability groups", where members have covenanted to share with each other what they believe God wants them to do and how they intend to do it, members may benefit from encouragement to think for themselves what Scripture has to say to them. This method does not begin with the Bible but with members' decisions.

Procedure

Each group member is invited to respond silently to the statement: One thing I believe God wants me to do this week is . . . After some quiet moments for reflection and decision, each one is encouraged to take the Bible and search for a verse or group of verses that either reinforces, encourages, challenges, or changes their intention. Allow five to fifteen minutes for this. After finding the verse or verses, they are to write down their intention in one declarative sentence: This week, God helping me, I intend to . . . because . . After time has been allowed for this, each member shares what they have written and adds: The verse(s) I have chosen for this week is (are) . . . because . . . No more than two questions may be asked of each person sharing, in order to ensure that everyone shares both their definite intention and their verse. After the first week, future meetings should have members sharing around four questions: What did I do last week in regard to my intention declared in this group? What do I intend to do this coming week? What Scripture am I using this week? What help do I need to accomplish my intention?

Key to success

O   The method works best with those who are exposed to regular Bible study and preaching, and who handle the text with some care and seriousness. People with no background in the Bible will find this difficult and some may use verses out of context.

20. DISCIPLINES AND DECISION: CHOOSING AND USING SPIRITUAL DISCIPLINES

Throughout the centuries Christians have practised a variety of personal and corporate spiritual disciplines as aids to faith and obedience. Some of these disciplines include daily prayer, daily study of Scripture, regular worship, tithing or financial sacrifice, fasting, keeping a journal or Christian diary, and service to the poor or needy.

A group which wants to encourage its members in the adoption and regular practice of one or more of these, or other, spiritual disciplines may wish to study the discipline as it appears in Scripture as well as in Christian tradition, in order to see who practised it and to what purpose.

Preparation

Decide which discipline the group wants to focus on. Using biblical tools, search the Scriptures for any instruction or examples given of the use of this discipline. Note all instances, and then choose those for the group to examine. Prepare a list of all passages to be studied.

Procedure

1. Give the group a list of the relevant passages and assign different passages to different people or to groups of two people. As people investigate their passages, have them ask: What is said about this discipline? What use of the discipline is present? Who uses it and why? What are the results, if shown? What teaching, warning, or help does this passage give to our practice of this discipline today?

2. Re-convene the whole group after ten to fifteen minutes. Ask each to share: What did you learn about this spiritual discipline? Allow for questions and free discussion. At some point, ask: Is anyone following this discipline at the present time? What is it like for you? At the conclusion of time allotted for this, ask: Would someone please summarize what we have learned? Is there anything we still need to learn about this before we try it individually? What would prevent any one of us from adopting it? Who is ready to try it?

Note Usually the group will not stop with a study of the biblical material but will want to find out what has been written about this discipline in contemporary and traditional writings as well. This needs to be planned for and resources sought out.

Keys to success

O   The group must be committed to at least a trial run of the discipline chosen so that experiential as well as intellectual learning can result.

O   Most disciplines are difficult to implement when new, and group members will need to support and encourage each other.

Resource

Celebration of Discipline, Richard J. Foster, Harper & Row, 1978.

7

Building Relationships in the Small Group

Positive personal relationships belong at the heart of any good small group. Human beings were created to live in relationship with God and with each other. We long to know and be known as the individual and unique people that we are, even as we fear involvement with others lest we be misunderstood, rejected or hurt. Simply sitting in a group with people does not guarantee the development of personal relationships which affirm personal worth and give a sense of caring and belonging. There are principles, skills and activities which facilitate good conversations, help people to know each other better, and build involvement and unity among group members. Understanding group dynamics, communication skills, and the use of sharing questions can help leaders and members to build the sense of community so important in group life.

GROUP DYNAMICS
Group dynamics can be approached from several different time perspectives:
○   What happens before the group "formally" begins.
○   What happens during the group meeting time.
○   What happens after the group ends and during the time before the next group meeting.

As the group gathers
Small groups do not begin after everyone has arrived, or all have taken a seat and the leader says, "Let's start." The small group actually begins when the second person enters the meeting room.

Each person who comes to the group should be welcomed warmly, greeted by name, chatted to for a few moments and made to feel as if someone has been waiting for them to come and looking forward to their presence. For this reason, the leader should make every effort to be one of the first people to arrive and should focus on people, not on last-minute arrangements. A host or hostess can take on the welcoming ministry, which should be relatively casual and informal. If refreshments have been prepared, they should be offered. Questions which ask how the week has gone, ask after family members, or about something that was shared during the previous meeting, all help to make the group member feel important. Anyone who was absent should be told that they were missed. Leaders should avoid spending the preliminary time talking to their own close friends and should seek to speak to newcomers or those not as well known in the group.

Seating

Seating arrangements are important to a good discussion. As far as possible, arrange the seating in a circle so that each person can easily see all the other members without having to turn physically in their direction. Minimize the distances between people so that they can see and hear each other with few distractions. Move the chairs close together in the circle. When people sit next to each other in a straight line, such as three on a sofa, they will usually find it difficult to see and talk to each other. Try to put only two people on a sofa, one in each corner facing inwards so they can see and converse easily. Seating should all be at the same level, not with some seated on the floor, for example, and some on chairs. Eye contact is difficult unless there are clear sight lines between members, with no lamps, flower arrangements or other intrusions. Seats should be comfortable and preferably have a back if the meeting is to last for any length of time.

Latecomers

Be prepared for latecomers. Groups are often uncertain about how to deal with latecomers. Do you wait for everyone to arrive before you begin? This may delay the meeting unduly. Do you stop the discussion when a latecomer enters? What about seating?

Have a plan. Begin the group at the pre-selected starting time or when a majority are present. If others are expected, have seating ready for them so that no one has to get up when they arrive. The leader should acknowledge the latecomer saying briefly, "Welcome . . . We were just doing . . ." and then continue. Long explanations or starting again should be avoided. Latecomers should not be ignored, but neither should they be given excessive attention. You hope they will come earlier next time.

During the meeting

Developing good patterns of participation in the group discussion is one of the most challenging and rewarding of all group activities. The goal should be to involve all members of the group so that no one person dominates the discussion and no one is ignored or excluded. The first meeting sets a pattern which is often continued throughout all the meetings of the group. If only two or three talk the first time, they are the only ones likely to talk freely in future meetings. If some do not talk at all at the first meeting, they begin to perceive themselves as silent members of the group and talk very little in future sessions. For this reason, among others, it is important to set a pattern during the first meeting in which everyone talks and no one dominates.

Sharing questions

One way to do this is to begin a new small group by asking a personal "sharing question''. This is a question which gives people permission to talk about themselves in a relatively safe way. The question should be one that can be answered easily by every member. This brief question can be answered in three or four sentences by each of the group in turn, for example: What are two things you can tell us about yourself that would help us to know you? Or: Tell us something about yourself. What is one main thing you do in your work and what is one thing you do for fun or enjoyment? Or: Tell us who you are and what you are hoping to get out of this group. Or: Who are you? Describe yourself in five key words or phrases.

Names

In a new group the use of names is very important. Many people cannot remember names if they do not see them written down. Large name tags or a sheet of paper passed around with all the names on it may be helpful during the first meeting. Someone has said that the sweetest sound in anyone's ear is the sound of his or her own name. The frequent use of names builds a sense of belonging and connectedness. Helping people to learn names quickly gives a sense of comfort and increases direct communication between group members. At the first meeting consider taking time to go round the circle and ask each person to begin a brief time of sharing by stating their name, spelling it aloud if it is unusual, answering a sharing question, and then repeating their name at the end of their time of talking. The leader should repeat and use names as often as possible.

Information sheet

Consider preparing an information sheet. Ask group members to write down their names and addresses with home phone numbers and any additional information desired, such as birthday or names and ages of children or place of work. Make a copy of this list available to each group member by the second meeting, so that members can get in touch with each other between meetings as well as learn a little bit about each other from the information sheet.

COMMUNICATION SKILLS

Communication in a group is a complex event. The complexities rise with the number of people involved and the intensity of the discussion. Communication is both verbal and non-verbal, conveying feelings as well as ideas, opinions, information and wishes. Communication occurs at different levels, as the group members grow in their trust of one another and in their willingness to talk about themselves in personal ways. A mark of growing cohesion and trust in a group is a deepening of the level of communication among the members.

Levels of communication

Level 1: Cliché conversation. This is the superficial chit-chat level of talking which focuses on safe topics such as the weather, sporting events, local happenings, etc. At this level people reveal only "safe" things about themselves which they would not mind having known as public information such as place of work, number of children, etc. The first minutes of any meeting will usually include this kind of conversation.

Level 2:   Sharing of information and facts. At this level people talk about events, ideas and facts, but not yet really about themselves. In a Bible study group people will feel most comfortable if questions can be clearly answered from the text and if they are not expected to express their own commitments and beliefs. Statements are usually made as generalizations and there is often some sense of "performance" present as some members wonder if they have the "right" answers, or are saying the right things.

Level 3:   Sharing of ideas and opinions. There is more willingness at this level to share one's own personal ideas and opinions. This takes a bit more risk. Members are becoming willing to share more information about themselves. As people talk more about themselves, they begin to know each other better. As people express ideas and opinions, differences emerge and members test the limits of diversity. If conflict is handled in a positive way, members will risk more honesty in the expression of their ideas.

Level 4:   Sharing of feelings. At this level people are willing to risk telling other group members what they are feeling, not just what they are thinking. These feelings may be positive or negative. A common phrase is "I feel . . ." Feelings are not disguised but expressed directly during the group meeting. This involves a signficant degree of trust. Members risk self-disclosure because they value the benefits of being known and knowing the other members. At this level members are less hidden and more open to each other.

Level 5:   Peak communication. This is the deepest level of communication when members experience strongly their sense of belonging and sharing with the other group members without defensiveness or barriers. Openness, transparency, and self-disclosure shapes the flow of the conversation. This level of intimacy is rare yet very powerful. Sometimes this depth of communication is experienced in a "filled" silence, where people sense oneness with each other beyond words.

Improving skills

Almost all small groups can strengthen the life of their group through improving communication. Basic communication skills in groups can be developed by both leaders and members. These include skills in listening, in advancing the discussion, and in talking. Good communication depends upon a willingness to listen actively, to involve fellow members, and to express your own ideas and feelings when appropriate. Often old patterns need to be broken so that new patterns of speaking and listening can develop. Here is a list of some of the most basic skills and, where appropriate, accompanying exercises that might be attempted as an aid to building good communication patterns in a group.

Skill 1:   Attending

This involves physically and emotionally focusing on the person who is speaking, so as to convey interest and your intention to listen.

Physically you turn so that you are facing the speaker as directly as possible. You establish eye-contact and, while not staring, you look directly at the person while she or he is speaking, without your reading or taking notes or thinking about something else. During the time the other is speaking, you convey non-verbally or in brief words or phrases that you are paying attention to what is being said. This includes responsive facial gestures such as smiling or questioning, an open posture which leans slightly towards the speaker and does not sit back with arms folded across the chest. It excludes distracting behaviour such as clicking pens, closing of eyes, or nervous tapping of fingers. Physical posture, expression and movement display interest or disinterest in what the other is saying.

"Door openers" are aids to conversation which use brief words like "Hmmm . . ." "Ahh . . ." "Yes," "Really?" or "How about that?" "What?" "No kidding!" "How interesting!" or "Tell us more." These brief phrases invite the speaker to continue talking, without introducing new material into the conversation and changing the focus of attention.

Whilst attending is very easy to do, many people in groups do not actually pay serious attention to what is being said by other group members. Sometimes this is because each one is busy preparing his or her own speech. To listen actively is hard work and an act of love which puts the other person in the centre for a while and grants that most precious of gifts – your undivided attention.

Exercise Divide into groups of three. Arrange the seating so that each can see and hear the others without strain. Look and see if each is physically turned towards the others or if some sit at an angle or with barriers in the way. Then take turns with one talking, the other attending, and the third observing. The talker should talk about: How I see myself as a communicator in this group, or: One thing that I get excited about or angry about. The attender should add no context, but only practise attending and keeping the talker talking. The observer should report after three minutes how each did. Then take turns so that all three perform each task. At the end, discuss: How could we improve our ability to attend in this group?

Skill 2: Information- and opinion-seeking

This is a very simple skill which every group member should use frequently to involve those who have not spoken recently in the group or whose ideas or opinions should be brought into the discussion. You do not have to wait for people to volunteer their ideas or feelings in the group. You can ask directly: John, what do you think (feel or know) about . . . ? Mary, I'd be interested in your opinion on . . . Who knows something about . . . ? Does anyone have an opinion on the importance of what you have noticed about . . . ? The use of names helps to bring people into the discussion. Care should be taken never to ask questions which the person will not be able to answer or which will embarrass them. In the Bible study, point to the verse with the answer in it as part of the question, for example: Bill, in verses 2 and 3, what do you think is the most important idea.

Skill 3: Clarification

In most conversations, things are said which are not fully understood by the listener. We often assume that we know what was intended by the speaker, so we make a guess about what was meant, react, and then continue the discussion. Misunderstandings, vagueness, and lack of clear thought often result. Many times in a conversation things are said which we may grasp generally but not precisely. Usually we ignore it and go on. In groups it is sometimes important to slow down the discussion to make sure that what people hear is what the speaker intends. Communication only exists when what is heard is understood in the same sense in which the speaker meant it. Sometimes the literal words are misheard. More often, the meaning is what is unclear.

Asking a question for clarification can help to clear up any possible confusion, misunderstanding, uncertainty or lack of clarity. It can also help the speaker to define more carefully or think through more competely just what was important in what was said.

Examples of clarification questions are: I'm not sure what you meant by . . . Could you restate that? Do you mean . . . ? Could you define that or give me an example? Could you repeat that and say a little more about what you mean? When you use the word . . . do you mean to say . . . ? Why is that important to you? Did you feel your question was answered? Do you think you have been understood? Have we got it right?

Exercise In any small group, have one person deliberately limit herself or himself for half an hour to asking only questions for clarification. Do not make any independent comments or offer opinions of your own. See what happens for the person and in the group.

Skill 4: Paraphrasing

Paraphrasing is one of the highest skills in listening because the listener attempts to play back to the speaker what has been said in his or her own words.

At its best, paraphrasing is not simply parroting or repeating exactly what has been said, but it is a restatement showing that careful listening has been attempted. It gives the listener an opportunity to "check with the speaker" to see if understanding has resulted. Good paraphrasing usually attempts to be sensitive to the feelings as well as the words which have been expressed.

One of the most common mistakes that people make in attempting to convey understanding or sympathy is to say: I know just how you feel because I've been through the same thing myself. This comment may do two undesirable things. First, it changes the focus of attention from the person who was talking to the new person who is now centre stage with their experience. Secondly, even when experiences are similar, they are not identical. People may feel cut off or discounted rather than affirmed when they hear "I know just how you feel." A better pattern is to ask questions of clarification in order to elicit a clearer understanding, and then attempt to paraphrase what has been heard from the other without talking about yourself.

Some examples are: This is what I heard you saying . . . Is that it? What you are saying is . . . Your struggle is . . . You mean . . . and you have strong feelings about that, haven't you? John, you've said . . . Helen, you've expressed the idea that . . . Mark, your central concern is . . . Tom, what you propose is . . . Ralph, your reactions are . . . It bothers you, Jane, that . . . Colin, your experience suggests that . . . You are feeling . . . What you want is . . . You believe that . . .

Exercise In a group of three, have one as speaker, one as paraphraser, one as observer. The speaker discusses: One concern I have for our group/church/ community/world is . . . or: One of the most important experiences of my life was . . . because . . . The paraphraser attempts to keep the conversation going as long as possible by using the skills of attending, clarifying, and paraphrasing. The observer reports on how it went after five minutes. Each one takes a turn at each part. At the conclusion, discuss the advantages and difficulties of using these skills.

Skill 5: Extending

This simple skill is used to build a "thought line" in a discussion.

After an answer is given to a question, or a comment is made, the leader can ask: Does anyone have anything to add to what has been said? Is there more that could be said about this subject? Have we left out anything important? Is there anything else that comes to mind?

Skill 6   Justifying

This skill involves asking people to give reasons for what they have said.

The assumption is that group members want to take seriously what is said as worthy of consideration. Sometimes suggestions are made which seem completely irrelevant to the discussion or tangential to the text. Occasionally members will make strong statements of opinion about which not everyone will agree. The discussion will be strengthened if people regularly are asked to give reasons to support their statements. This should be done in a positive, non-argumentative way. Justifying helps the group to stay on the subject and not to jump around to lots of different topics.

Some examples are: Where do you find that in the text? What in the text suggested that to you? Why do you make that statement? We were talking about . . . and you suggested . . What is the connection between what we were discussing and your comment? What reasons do you have that support what you are saying? Why do you say that? How do you support that conclusion?

Skill 7:   Re-directing

This skill is particularly important for leaders when group members continue to address all their questions and comments to the leader rather than to other group members.

When a question is asked of the leader, the leader can turn to one of the group members and say: I'd be interested in what Tom has to say about that. Tom, how would you answer that? When comments seem too much directed at one person, that person can involve two other people in discussion by saying: Tom, what do you think about what Sue has said? The leader must take care not to respond to everything said in the group or the group will not become truly interactive. It helps if the leader does not speak after each person and does not re-state or summarize everything that has been said.

Re-directing, with the use of names, encourages members to talk with each other, not just with the leader. The image is that of a person to whom a ball has been thrown. As quickly as possible throw the ball to a group member who has not had the ball recently, and encourage members to throw the ball to each other, not just to the leader. This makes for a much more exciting discussion.

Skill 8:   "I" messages instead of "You" messages

Communication in the group improves when members are willing to take responsibility for their own ideas and feelings and use the personal pronoun "I".

To say "I feel" or "I think" is much more direct and helpful than "Some people think . . ." or "Some believe . . ." When expressing a feeling, idea or opinion, try saying "I" instead of "You". For example, "I am discouraged with our group's progress" rather than "You are wasting the group's time." Being willing to share directly what you think or feel rather than talking about others or hiding behind the generality or vagueness of "People say . . ." can make a vast difference in the vitality of a group. Using "I" to express personal feelings directly can deepen the level of communication in the group. Shared feelings build trust. Concealed feelings or indirect messages can sabotage the group.

Skill 9: The personal implication question

When discussions seem too general, vague or abstract, it can help to ask a personal implication question to help focus the conversation to become more direct and specific. Questions like this are usually asked towards the middle and end of a group discussion after some general thoughts have been shared.

Some examples are: What is your own opinion about that? How would the decision we are considering affect you personally? How important is what you are saying to you personally? How much does this matter to you? Is what we are discussing anything that anyone has struggled with particularly? Does it make any real difference to anyone here whether we go this way or that way? Have you struggled with this issue yourself? Has anything like this ever happened to you? Does this match anybody's own experience? Is that true for you in your situation? How likely do you consider that possibility to be? Would you yourself want to do what you are suggesting? Is that something you yourself believe? Is this happening in your life now?

Questions like this should not be asked in a hostile or threatening way but as a low-keyed exploration of reality.

Skill 10: Handling talkative and silent members

Excessively talkative or silent members can both be dealt with through an understanding of seating arrangements, non-verbal communication and group dynamics.

Research indicates that people seated directly opposite the discussion leader are most likely to talk. Those seated right next to the leader are least likely to talk, because it is harder for the leader to maintain eye contact with them. When someone consistently talks too much, consider changing the seating arrangements so that he or she sits next to the leader. Put the silent member opposite the leader where eye contact can be maintained easily.

Other tips: Break eye contact with the over-talkative and look persistently at other members of the group. When the person pauses in the midst of an over-long speech, be quick to break in and say, "I'd like to hear from someone who hasn't spoken yet." If the talker continues to dominate, stop using open questions and put all questions to particular people, using their names first. For example: Jim, what do you think is meant in verse 2? Sue, do you have anything to add to what Jim has said? Mark, how about you? If all else fails, talk to the person outside the group. Share your concern that all members of the group have a good opportunity to talk and ask for the person's help in achieving this goal. Be aware that sometimes people talk too much in a group because they are not certain that anyone takes them seriously. Active listening both within and outside the group context can be helpful in breaking a destructive pattern. Do not allow an over-talkative member to take over a group. It is not fair to the other group members. Act in love, but act!

The silent member should be encouraged to more active participation by picking up on non-verbal cues. Watch the silent member until they seem ready to say something as indicated by posture or facial expression. Then call on them. Talking with them before and after the group is also helpful. Asking sharing questions which are non-threatening may be very important so that the quieter member has a time to talk. Do not force people to talk who may need to be quiet in the group. Give them a chance to participate but allow them freedom if they need it.

SHARING QUESTIONS

A very good tool to help build relationships in a Bible study group is to use a sharing question at each group meeting. These are one or two sentence questions which invite people to tell the group something about themselves. It gives people permission to talk about themselves in a structured context where all share something and all listen to the others. These are not questions which ask for knowledge, information or opinions about issues but questions which encourage people to talk about themselves – their past experiences, present situations, hopes for the future, joys and sorrows, struggles and successes. The stress is not on sharing ideas or concepts but on sharing ourselves. The sharing question is used to help members to move beyond chit-chat and shallow conversation to tell something about themselves to help other members of the group get to know them. Usually the question is asked at the beginning of the meeting time and takes between twenty and thirty minutes for all to answer.

Sharing questions can be thought of in terms of five main categories:
O   Past
O   Present
O   Future
O   Affirmation
O   Accountability.

Past tense sharing questions

These questions ask people to share something about their personal history.

Examples
O   Where did you live when you were twelve years old, and what is one strong memory you have from that time?
O   Who was the most influential person in your childhood, and why?
O   What was the most memorable holiday you ever took, and why?
O   When, if ever, did God become more than a word to you, and how did that happen?
O   What is one experience of success that you can remember, and what did it mean to you?
O   What is one quality from your parents that you wanted to keep, and anything you wished you could change?
O   When was the first time you heard about Jesus, and what did you think about him?
O   When did you meet your spouse, and what do you remember from that time?
O   What were the Christmas holidays like for you when you were growing up, and how did you feel about them?
O   What has been your most important spiritual experience?
O   What was your relationship to a church as you grew up, and how did you feel about it?
O   What was the most exciting (challenging, difficult, growth-producing, enjoyable, or terrible) part of your life up to now, and why?

These past tense questions are especially appropriate in the early stages of a new group and when new members join. By inviting people to share their past, we begin to know something about the influences and experiences that have helped to make us who we are.

Present tense sharing questions

These questions invite people to discuss what is happening in their lives at the present time. The very recent past may be a part of these questions, but the focus is on the experiences and feelings that are part of daily life now.

Examples

○　What do you do on a typical Tuesday? When do you get up, what do you do during the day, and when do you go to bed?

○　What is one part of your life that you enjoy, and one part that is difficult for you?

○　What is your favourite spot in your home or garden, and why?

○　What is a good thing happening in your life right now, and what makes it good?

○　What do you like to do for fun?

○　When you have some free time to yourself, what do you like to do?

○　What is one thing that you worried about or struggled with this past week?

○　What are you looking forward to, and what are you reluctant to face, during the next week?

○　What is one decision facing you that you find difficult, and why?

○　What is a satisfying relationship and/or a frustrating relationship in your life, and what makes it so?

○　When do you struggle with yourself and win, or when do you struggle with yourself and lose? How do you feel about that?

○　What is the most important or most meaningful or most satisfying thing that you do in a week, and why?

○　What is one thing that gave you joy or a sense of accomplishment this week?

○　What is one thing you are proud of about yourself?

○　What is one thing you are good at, and one thing you are bad at?

○　Where are you changing or growing in your life, and what helps and what hinders that process?

○　What spiritual discipline do you find the easiest or the most difficult?

○　What do you like about your job, and is there anything you find boring?

　　　Present tense questions help us to talk about what is going on in our lives right now. Often group members do not know what fellow members od in their daily lives or how they feel about what is happening to them unless such questions are asked.

Future tense sharing questions

These questions focus on what is ahead, usually not in the near future but a little further off. They help people to talk about their desires for change, their hopes and dreams, expectations and possibilities. Questions of this type are usually asked after a group has been together for a while.

Examples

○　If you knew you could not fail, and money was no problem, what one thing would you like to do in the next five years?

○　If you could change one thing about yourself or develop one quality that you do not now have, what would it be?

○　What is one relationship you would like to strengthen, and what steps could you take to develop it?

O   What would be the perfect holiday for you? Where would it be, and what would you do?

O   If you could change one thing about the world, what would it be and why?

O   If you could be doing anything you wanted to this time next year, what would it be?

O   If you could accomplish one positive change for good in our church, what would it be? How might you go about it?

O   If you went home and found a cheque written to you for one million pounds, how would you spend the money?

O   What would you like to have said about you at your funeral?

O   How do you want your children to remember you, and what are you doing to ensure those memories?

O   What is one change you would like to make in your life in the next two years, and why?

O   What is one dream or hope you have for the future?

O   What is one anxiety you have about the future, and how do you deal with it?

Affirmation questions

These are questions which invite group members to say positive things about each other. Often we form friendships which are meaningful to us but we seldom say out loud to the other people just what they mean to us and why we value them. During the last meetings of a group, affirmation becomes particularly appropriate.

Examples

O   What is one quality that you value or admire in one or more members of this group?

O   If you could give a special gift to each member of the group, what would it be and why?

O   What spiritual gifts do you see present in one or more members of this group? How are those gifts being used in a helpful way?

O   What has been meaningful to you in this group?

O   How has this group been important or helpful to you?

O   What do you value especially about this group?

O   If you were called on to give a speech describing the good qualities of the members of this group, what would you say?

While group members are often reticent to say positive things about each other, it is a quality that can often be seen in the life of Jesus and the apostles. They could see the qualities in people and affirm those, thus helping people to recognize and value what God was doing within and through them. This type of affirmation can be very important in expressing feelings and in building a sense of belonging and being cared for.

Accountability questions

These questions are asked when group members promise to work actively at living out the implications of their Christian faith. Such questions should only be asked when people have chosen to make themselves accountable to fellow group members.

Examples

○ What do you believe God wants you to do this week, and when, and how do you intend to do it?

○ What changes do you believe you should make in your habits or actions this week? How will you tackle these?

○ What Christian action will you attempt this week, and what help will you need to accomplish it?

○ What spiritual disciplines are you going to follow this week, and why?

○ How did you get on with your commitment from last week?

○ What success and what failure have you experienced this week in your attempt to follow Christ?

○ What relationship should you work on this week, and how will you do it?

○ How will you practise thankfulness to God this week?

○ How is the Spirit prompting you as a result of our Bible study? What will you do about it, and when?

○ How will you share the good news of the gospel this week, and with whom?

○ What prayer discipline do you intend to observe this week?

○ What is one responsibility that you have to fulfil this week and how do you feel about it?

Guidelines for using sharing questions

○ Ask the question and call on someone to answer who will be comfortable with the question. If you can be brief, answer the question yourself first as an example for the others. If the first one or two sharing talk for too long, suggest that the others answer the question more briefly so that everyone will have a chance to share.

○ Allow people to pass if they cannot or do not want to answer the question. After all have shared, however, go back to any who passed and ask if they would like to share now. Many times they will, and to ignore them will leave them feeling left out. Never force people to share. Do not embarrass or manipulate people. While encouraging everyone to participate, allow them to re-shape the question if it makes them feel more comfortable. Move quickly on to the next person or the next activity.

○ Go round in a circle to answer the question, taking only a few moments for each one to share. Do not ask questions of the speaker or it will not be possible for everyone to get an opportunity to talk. The purpose is to help us know each other better, not to explore in depth the particular topic or experience.

○ Match the threat level or intensity level of the question to the willingness and experience of the group members. Start with relatively safe questions which anyone can answer without much thought or difficulty. As the group continues, risk asking slightly more threatening questions which call for more self-disclosure and more thoughtful reflection.

○ Ask open-ended questions which cannot be answered "yes" or "no" and which can be answered by every member of the group. Do not ask, for example, "When and how did you become a Christian?" if not everyone has had that experience or uses that kind of language. Do not ask, "Where did you go to college and what was your field of study?" if anyone in the group did not go to college. Be sensitive to the backgrounds of the group members, and do not ask questions that only a few can answer. The purpose of a sharing question is to help each of the group members to talk briefly about himself or herself.

O   Do not ask questions that call for ideas or opinions on controversial issues or problems of the day. You are interested in people's experiences and their feelings about those experiences. During the Bible study time, you will have plenty of opportunity to discuss ideas. The sharing time is for meeting each other at the personal level.

O   Do not ask questions which require people to confess their sins or say only negative things about themselves. When confession occurs, it should be voluntary not coerced. Do not ask: What is your worst fault? Try to balance the opportunity to mention positive as well as difficult things. Asking questions which require everyone to share their victories can be just as demoralizing as asking them to concentrate always on their imperfections and shortcomings. Not: What was your great success in answered prayer this week? But perhaps: What has been a high and low in your experience of prayer?

Sharing questions are such a helpful tool that most groups will want to consider using them at almost all meetings even after they have been together for many months. More simple invitations to share can also be used, such as: Does anyone have anything they want to share? Or: Let's take some time and catch up. What's been happening in your life this week? If used too frequently, such general questions tend to encourage repetitive sharing rather than opening new opportunities to know each other in different aspects of our lives.

After the group

After the group meeting ends, remember that the group is not over until the last person goes home.

Often the most significant conversations will occur after the group time is finished. The leader should make every effort to stay around and talk until everyone has gone home. Sometimes questions or concerns which could not be expressed in the group will come up in the after-meeting. Someone with a question about their relationship with Jesus Christ may linger for a word of counsel. Those with a decision or problem may ask for prayer or help. Good listening is very important at this key time. Lives may be encouraged, directed or helped by these conversations. Take them seriously.

When possible, a contact with group members between meetings can be very worthwhile in strengthening the relationships in the group. When some of the members can be together socially, or when telephone conversations occur between members, the sense of connectedness and caring grows. Some groups adopt a discipline of each one talking with at least one other group member during the week to share prayer concerns, or have a meal together, or just to get to know each other better. Arranging a social time when all the members of the group can participate is a delightful way to build a sense of community. Planning a picnic in a nearby park can involve children and family members not regularly in the group. Playing a group game of soccer or going to the theatre or a concert knits people together. Even as simple a thing as going on a group walk or hike can help people to get to know each other in ways seldom possible during a typical group meeting. Many groups benefit from "playing" together as well as studying and praying together.

PRAYER IN THE SMALL GROUP

Prayer in the small group can be a wonderful or a terrifying experience. People who have never prayed out loud may panic when told that they are expected to pray, or that prayers will be offered by everyone going around the circle. People who have only heard formal prayers in church may suspect that all prayers must be long, cover many topics, and include a great deal of spiritual language and special phrases. Group prayer under such circumstances and with such expectations can be a most uncomfortable experience.

On the other hand many groups report that the most meaningful part of their life together is the time spent in prayer. In such groups people have learned how to pray with each other, and they find their sense of the presence and power of God enhanced by the group experience. Many small groups carefully allot the last thirty minutes of all meetings for a relaxed, informal time of praying together.

Conversation with God

One helpful way to think of prayer in the small group is as conversation with God. The prayer time is not a time for religious speeches but rather a time of realizing and enjoying the presence of God. Conversation with any person usually includes both listening and speaking and tends to focus upon only one topic at a time. In conversation with God, it is entirely appropriate that there be times of silence as well as times of spoken prayer. When prayer is offered aloud, it is usually limited to one topic at a time and expressed in only a few sentences. Sometimes groups even find it helpful to offer prayers of one word to God.

A pattern for prayer

If your group includes people who do not feel comfortable with group prayer, you may want to introduce the following pattern which many groups have found helpful. The first week the leader opens the meeting with a brief prayer of one or two sentences expressing thanks to God and acknowledging his presence. Towards the end of the meeting time, the leader explains that one of the purposes of the group is to learn to pray together. No one will be forced to pray, but the hope is that we may discover the value of prayer together. During this first prayer time the group will focus on expressing thanks to God. This may be done in silence or group members may want to offer one word or one sentence prayers of thanks. If people want to pray more than once, that is all right. After a few moments the leader will close with an Amen.

The next week, before the prayer time the leader suggests that this week the group may want to consider a four step pattern for group prayer. The four steps are:

1. **Jesus is here.** In this stage we remember the promise of Jesus in Matthew 18.20 that where two or three are gathered in his name, there he is in their midst. During this stage of prayer, we quietly focus on Jesus and recognize the presence of Christ with us in this place. We remember the love of God, his goodness and why he is worthy of adoration and gratitude.

2. **Thank you, Lord.** In this stage we remember all that God has done for us and we offer him our thanks.

3. **Help me, Lord.** In this stage we acknowledge our own need and remember the biblical promise: "Leave all your worries with him, because he cares for you." (1 Peter 5.7) We may confess our sin and our shortcomings or make a specific

request. We seek to be honest, and as we pray for ourselves, others can pray with us to support us.

4. **Help my brother; help my sister.** In this final stage of prayer we pray for each other. This is an act of love. We may begin by praying for those sitting to the right or to the left of us. We may pray for each other by name or for those outside the group in need of God's love and help. These requests can be brief, but wherever possible we will try to pray for each member of the group.

Tell the group that you will lead them in a time of prayer following this pattern. You will pray first in a single sentence expressing your own prayer. Others are invited to join in as they would like. As you move to each new step, they are invited to pray, using the key phrase as a help. They may pray in silence or out loud as they wish. Encourage prayers of one or two sentences only. Say that you will close the prayer time with an Amen.

Do not go round the circle to pray. This puts enormous pressure on people, and some will not return to a group where they have felt coerced to "take a turn" in prayer. While some like to hold hands during prayer as a symbol of unity, others may find this distracting. Some groups have an open time of prayer and then close the time by holding hands and praying the Lord's prayer together.

Other patterns

Other patterns of prayer may be helpful. Some people benefit from writing down brief prayers and then reading them in the group. Some groups allow a five or ten minute time of silent prayer where the group is quiet together before the Lord, before a final summary prayer is offered. Some may ask one or two members in advance to come prepared to lead the group in prayer. Whatever pattern is chosen, it is important that enough time is allowed for prayer if it is to be included in the group. One minute tacked on at the end is not likely to be particularly meaningful.

A common problem arises when groups spend all their time sharing prayer requests and end up with almost no time for actual prayer. It is better to begin praying and allow people to express their concerns in prayer than to fill the time with more discussion. When a person is prayed for, or a concern mentioned, others may express support for the prayer request by also praying.

Particularly meaningful prayer can result from a good Bible study which concludes with the question: What can we learn from this passage to help us in our praying? Sometimes groups fall into repetitive habits of praying as, for example, when they pray only for the sick. A broader vision and practice of prayer can be informed by Scripture. The basic aspects of prayer as seen in Scripture should become a regular part of the group's prayer life. These are adoration, thanksgiving, confession, commitment, and intercession. Following the pattern of the Lord's Prayer reminds us of our unity as we pray, "Our Father . . ." and should influence the kinds of things for which we pray.

Unity

Prayer can unify a group as nothing else will. To experience unity in Christ through prayer can be a life-changing experience. It is worth the initial awkwardness to learn how to pray together because so much benefit can come from it. In Christian small groups we study the Bible because we believe that through it God speaks to us. Through prayer, the dialogue is completed as we speak to God. Good Bible study begins and ends in prayer.

Epilogue

We began this book by celebrating the possibilities of life together in a Christian small group which uses the Bible as a resource. When all the methods of study have been examined and all the dynamics of group life have been explored, it is important to remember that Christian community exists first of all because of the loving action of God on our behalf. We come together in response to his gracious invitation through the power of the Holy Spirit at work in us.

In small groups, as in all of the Christian life, we live by grace and are not driven or dominated by law, even the "laws" of group dynamics. The methods and principles which have been suggested here should never be seen as ends in themselves but only as possible resources to aid in the building of authentic Christian community. Where they are helpful, use them. When they impede the growth of learning and love in a group, put them aside.

Too much attention on methodology may frighten the beginner or lay person who feels the need to master all of the material and do things "just right". It is encouraging to note that most small groups display remarkable abilities to overcome the limitations and shortcomings of their leaders and members. They flourish even when functioning under less than ideal conditions.

Remember the promise of Jesus that "where two or three come together in my name, I am there with them." All new ventures involve some risk of moving into the unknown. It is confidence in the promised presence of Christ in our midst which draws us together in the adventure of faith.

Subject Index

Index of Bible References

Bibliography

Aids for Group Bible Study

Coleman, Lyman. Search the Scriptures series. Rev. ed. *Encyclopedia of Serendipity*. A Bible study series for youth groups is also available. Published by Serendipity House, Box 1012, Littleton, CO 80160.

Discover Your Bible, Inc., 941 Wealthy S.E., Box 6252, Grand Rapids, MI 49506. Bible study guides designed for use in churches with a Reformed perspective.

Fisherman Bible Study Guides, published by Harold Shaw Publishers, Box 567, Wheaton, IL 60186. Inductive studies for neighborhood, student, and church groups.

Inter-Varsity Bible Study Guides, Inter-Varsity Press, Box F, Downers Grove, IL 60515. A series of discussion Bible study guides, some topical and others focused on a particular book.

Neighborhood Bible Studies, Box 222, Dobbs Ferry, NY 10522. Each guide consists of a series of questions designed for inductive group Bible study. Guides are available for almost all books in the Old Testament and New Testament.

Aids for Leaders of Bible Study Groups

Gibson, William. *A Covenant Group for Lifestyle Assessment* (Participant's Manual). Rev. ed. The United Presbyterian Church U.S.A. Program Agency, 1981. Order directly from PCUSA, Office of Social Education, Room 1101, 475 Riverside Drive, New York, NY 10115.

Griggs, Donald and Patricia. *Generations Learning Together*. Abingdon Press, 1976.

Hunt, Gladys. *How-to Handbook for Inductive Bible-Study Leaders*. Harold

Shaw Publishers, 1971.

Kunz, Marilyn, and Catherine Schell. *How to Start a Neighborhood Bible Study*. Neighborhood Bible Studies (Box 222, Dobbs Ferry, NY 10522), 1966.

Navigators. *The Small Group Letter*. A newsletter published by NavPress, P.O. Box 6000, Colorado Springs, CO 80934.

Nyquist, James. *Leading Bible Discussions*. Inter-Varsity Press, 1967.

Richards, Lawrence. *69 Ways to Start a Study Group and Keep It Growing*. 2nd ed. Zondervan Publishing House, 1980.

VandeGriend, Al, and Neva Evenhouse. *Evangelism Through Bible Discovery Groups*. Discover Your Bible (P.O. Box 6252, Grand Rapids, MI 49506), 1979.

Wald, Oletta. *The Joy of Discovery in Bible Study*. Rev. ed. Augsburg Publishing House, 1975.

_____. *The Joy of Teaching Discovery Bible Study*. Augsburg Publishing House, 1976.

Helpful Books on Small Groups

Bangham, William. *Journey Into Small Groups*. Lay Renewal Press (1548 Poplar Avenue, Memphis, TN 38104), 1974.

Cosby, Gordon. *Handbook for Mission Groups*. The Potter's House (1658 Columbia Road N.W., Washington, DC 20009), 1975.

Denning, Dennis. *We Are One in the Lord: Developing Caring Groups in the Church*. Abingdon Press, 1982.

Evans, Louis H., Jr. *Covenant to Care*. Victor Books, 1982.

Griffin, Em. *Getting Together: A Guide for Good Groups*. Inter-Varsity Press, 1982.

Johnson, David W., and Frank P. Johnson. *Joining Together: Group Theory and Group Skills*. 2nd ed. Prentice-Hall, 1982.

Williamson, David L. *Group Power: How to Develop, Lead, and Help Groups Achieve Goals*. Prentice-Hall, 1982.